The Position of Magic
in Selected Medieval Spanish Texts

The Position of Magic in Selected Medieval Spanish Texts

By

Francis Tobienne, Jr.

Cambridge Scholars Publishing

The Position of Magic in Selected Medieval Spanish Texts, by Francis Tobienne, Jr.

This book first published 2008 by

Cambridge Scholars Publishing

15 Angerton Gardens, Newcastle, NE5 2JA, UK

British Library Cataloguing in Publication Data
A catalogue record for this book is available from the British Library

ISBN (10): 1-84718-496-0, ISBN (13): 9781847184962

To the Tobienne family and friends; specifically, my mother who passed on the gift of reading well; my father, who instilled within me a genuine, responsible work ethic and drive; my brother, who taught me to take risks; and to Alexis E. Ramsey, Gilmer C. Cook, Ernest L. Gibson III, Jeffrey L. Jones et al. (you **know** why). Lastly, to Jesus—my hero.

TABLE OF CONTENTS

Acknowledgments viii
Preface ix
Abstract xi

Chapter One 1
Introduction
1.1 Language & Semantics: Signification and Ambiguity of Terms
1.2 *Black* and *White*: Stories of Gray in Tales of *Miracula* and *Maleficium*
1.3 *Etymologiae*: Isidoran Application & the Classical Value of a Pre-history
1.4 A Quasi-Digression: a Pre-Modern Observation on Early Spanish Magic & *Naturalis*

Chapter Two 35
Introduction
2.1 A *Birth* of the University & "Caves" of Learning in Spain
2.2 The Position of Translation & Translation Centers in Spain
2.3 Alfonso X, *el Sabio*: Life, *Las Siete Partidas* and *el Lapidario*

Chapter Three 75
Introduction
3.1 Spanish Literature: A History of Ideas
3.2 Christian Magic: a Literary Exchange in the Explanation of Phenomena
3.3 Magic, *Miracula* & Mimesis

References 109
Author Biography 115

ACKNOWLEDGEMENTS

The author would like to thank first and foremost my Chair and Thesis Committee members Shaun F.D. Hughes, Clayton D. Lein, and Michael A. Ryan for their combined laser-like examining eye, patience as well as their respect—I am truly honored to be in and under such company. I would like to also thank the Purdue University Libraries, Phillips Academy-Andover Oliver Wendell Holmes (OWHL) Library, and the Harvard University Widener Library for their research and reading space[s] where I found myself surrounded by books, articles, and friendly dust mites. Further, I would like to thank Dr. Richard Kieckhefer at Northwestern University for his outside readership suggestions and comments. Lastly, I would like to thank those who questioned me at coffee shops, in the halls of Heavilon Hall, en route to my classes, et cetera; your interest in my project ensured that perhaps I was on the right track, and reflected—where future projects merit—continued research; specifically, thank you to the Medieval Studies program at Purdue University and its outstanding faculty and *Comitatus*; thank you to Room 215, located in Heavilon Hall, and to those indifferent to my subject—I can only hope to be relevant to you one day. If I may, I would like to challenge myself, that in those years to come, in addition to this present project, I might hope to become just a little wiser, a little more patient, and as strong a scholar as those that were present at my committee defense; this book is an indication that I am heading in their direction, and moreover—they need, of course, no absolution for the shortcomings that remain.

PREFACE

The subject of magic and its study on the Iberian Peninsula differs considerably from observing magic as a mere object of inquiry. For this particular project, I am concerned with the *subject* of magic as it existed as a viable, intellectual pursuit of examination alongside other liberal arts and sciences such as: philosophy, mathematics, astrology, alchemy and even religion; specifically, Samuel Waxman in his *Chapters on Magic in Spanish Literature*, suggests that "*It* ["magic," my emphasis] was even sometimes classed as one of the seven liberal arts" (1). Though this project does not concern directly the *Trivium* and the *Quadrivium*, the bifurcated headings of the seven liberal arts, "magic" was still taught alongside these dual distinctions and supported what one historian called, "a canonical way of depicting the realms of higher learning." In sum, magic became a way, and perhaps an association toward, an epistemological end.

Further, the goal of this project is to define and represent the ambiguity of magic and the tolerance of its expression in literature as its "definition" oscillated between religion and science; this medium exists within the literary exchange of Spanish Medieval Literature and its culture (the elements that aggregate into and express quasi-knowledge of a type of Spanish society). By examination, magic appears as the connection between religion and science, between belief (and belief systems) and praxis, or theory in practice regarding natural philosophy. Moreover, magic exists in the bifurcation of terms—*white* and *black* magic; the former has been closely linked in the thirteenth century as coinciding with *mirabilia* and *miracula*, or that which pertains to miracles, and the latter appears as— "black" or dark magic (*nigromancia*). As the increase of the dark arts became more prevalent, the Church retaliated by instituting its own version of magic, or explanations of supernatural phenomena. Still, the term *miracles* would do, and the practice, according to Jennifer Corry, was conceived as "white" magic. However, as we shall see such distinctions were not always easily ascertained. For example, the literature that captured such ambiguities best came from Spain in the form of the post-Aristotelian ideation of didactic and mimetic poetry. Spain had become Christian (albeit of the Arian variety) during the Visigoth Conquest (fifth century) but became a center of learning after the Muslim Conquest and Muslim, Christian and Jewish learning flourished there especially between the tenth

to the thirteenth centuries; Spain was the translating center for much science
and the philosophy of ideas; i.e. Spain became a center for the translating of
Arabic and Greek works into Latin, and then into Spanish. For this project I
will concern myself primarily with the Spanish texts either in translation
from the Arabic or Latin, and provide translations as necessary. I have
privileged specific Medieval Spanish texts that attempt to showcase the
aforementioned: the blurred lines of religion and science when magic is
overt, or occult in its illicit manifestations; as found within the Medieval
Spanish poetry of *Auto de Los Reyes Magos* and *Vida de Santa Maria
Egipciaca*, respectively.

Before each chapter is a brief account of that particular chapter heading,
followed by subsequent headings under that chapter. Again, the chapter-by-
chapter analysis collectively informs the reader that the study of magic in
thirteenth century Spain, and Spain's acceptance of such aberrant practices
(held so by the Church) that at times border on the comical, via the authorial
intent of Spanish Literature. When compared and taken alongside, a vast
survey of Literature ranging from the works of Saint Augustine to Alfonso
X, the Iberian Peninsula demonstrates, albeit pre-Inquisition and witch craze
(fifteenth thru the end of the seventeenth century), an acceptance of behavior
regarding magic and its derivative practice[s] such as astrology, *medicine*,
and sorcery; together, such behaviors served an explanatory role of the
natural and super/supra-natural realm.

ABSTRACT

The position of "magic" as it existed in thirteenth century Spain "articulated," via post-Aristotelian philosophical ideals, a rather subjective definition regarding the explanation of phenomena; "magic," seemingly fit within the categories of religion and science, albeit such distinctions were further problematized as the subject of magic's bifurcation received attention—namely, "black" magic and "white" magic; the former suggests the art of dark and demonic influence[s]; the latter concerns this project in particular as *mirabilia* and *miracula*—are examined in two poetic, Medieval Spanish accounts—the *Auto de Los Reyes Magos* and the *Vida de Santa María Egipciaca*. Here, magic relies on divine agency. Further, this project examines the literature that extends from Saint Augustine to Isidore of Seville and Alfonso X, el Sabio [or, the Wise]. It is the hope that this thesis, a launching pad for a larger work, may address the often blurred line[s] between such dual parallels as "magic and religion" as well as "magic and science." Where discussion of either religion or science enters, I argue, that "magic," the subjective explanation of phenomena in the suspension of the natural order[s], may in fact act as an axis point, or "gateway" into such a discursive praxis.

CHAPTER ONE

To begin, Chapter 1 briefly argues for an abridged history of *white* and *black* magic framed as a dialogical survey beginning with Saint Augustine and progressing toward the distinct voices of Stuart Clark, Karen L. Jolly and Jennifer M. Corry; moreover, such bifurcated distinctions involving magic are separated via the source or well-spring of power.[1] A definition of "magic" will be developed between these bifurcated terms and their particular application via examples of "Science" and "Religion," or an amalgam of these two belief systems.

A Rhetoric of Witchcraft, taken from Stuart Clark's massive text, *Thinking with Demons*, will be applied to a tangential Rhetoric of magic of sorts in both the oral and written tradition, and will be utilized when discussing the primary texts, *Auto de Los Reyes Magos* (*Auto*) and *Vida de Santa María Egipcíaca* (*Vida*) as well as the Latin treatise on magic known as the *Picatrix*. I am aware of the copious works written in Spain during the thirteenth century such as the *Libro De Alexandre, Berceo, Libro De Apolonio, Calila E Dimna, Poema De Fernán González*, and of course the *Gran Conquista De Ultramar*. These works interlace magic within a poetic framework, and have been dealt with in detail in the work of Antonio Garrosa Resina, but I have chosen the *Auto* and the *Vida* because these texts describe the affectation of magic in both religious belief and in applied science (Astrology); what is more, these texts exist as didactic and mimetic

---

[1] For this project I am well aware of the literature and philosophy of the post structuralist and socio-historical critic Michel Foucault with regard to the subject of power and the respective power structures that exist to express and suppress this ideation; however, I am not referring to power in the Foucauldian and policing sense per se, but the distinction between Divine and D[evil]ish influence. The former concerns miracles and serves God, while the latter concerns demonic control and serves Satan; both have their place and rely on each other for clarification and perhaps even existence. As one critic has noted, a theology of angels can only exist and is made possible via a theology involving demons. For further reading on the subject, though later than our scope of the thirteenth century, see Walter Stephens' *Demon Lovers: Witchcraft, Sex, and the Crisis of Belief* (Chicago: University of Chicago Press, 2002), especially chapters 3 thru 5, 10-11, 13. Stephens' accounts on the incubus and succubus are especially interesting and concern the subject of witchcraft from 1430-1530.

written forms. Moreover, upon the examination of such forms, magic as explanation of phenomena seems to blur the line between religion and science—respectively; specifically, the position of Divine agency via a human vessel as well as the "science" of the stars, or Astrology; arguably then, creating a parallel existence between magic and religion as well as magic and science.[2] Seemingly then, one could argue that to "understand" religion (belief and belief systems) and science in the thirteenth century, one must also take into consideration, and enter through the gates of *magic*.[3] What is more, I chose the following Medieval Spanish primary and anonymous texts: *Los Reyes Magos*, *Vida de Santa María Egipciaca*, and supplementary texts such as the *Picatrix*, the *Lapidario* and *Los Siete Partidas*, of Alfonso X, *el Sabio* (the Wise, or the Learned One), which, taken together, provide commentary on thirteenth century medieval Spanish culture and the court of Castile-León.

---

[2] An interesting work by Marcel Mauss, translated from the French into the English by Robert Brain, *A General Theory of Magic* (New York: Norton Co., 1972), examines the role of magic and the magician in the varied cultural landscapes that cater to its alignment with religion and science. At one point Mauss states:

> Words such as religion and magic, prayer and incantation, sacrifice and offering, myth and legend, god and spirit are interchanged indiscriminately. The science of religion has no scientific terminology […] However, our aim is not only to define words, but to set up natural classes of facts and, once we have established them, to attempt an analysis which will be as explanatory as possible. (7)

Mauss in making the attempt to disentangle such word and language uses to explain what he suggests *magic* to be, namely a "social phenomenon," does so at the risk of over-theorizing. Still, the small volume is helpful to our study of magic and religion, especially his fourth chapter, "An Analysis and Explanation of Magic". Here, he is concerned with magic being "continuous in nature" and its "efficacity" (91). Further, magic is believed and "like religion, is viewed as a totality" (92). In explaining magic, Mauss entangles his own rhetoric with that of a religious nature, and in fact suggests in an earlier place via influence of Frazer that religion stems from imperfect magic. Again, this is an intriguing investigation into the alignment of magic and religion. Lastly, in describing the "genuineness of magic," Mauss posits, with respect to the magician that: "Indeed, his faith is sincere in so far as it corresponds to the faith of the whole group…magic is believed and not perceived" (97).

[3] By no means am I strictly suggesting that we interchange the syntax of Religion with the syntax of magic, or the syntax of Science; i.e. terms such as the science of religion, or even religious magic, though they may exist, are highly dubious. Still, there is something to be said in disentangling each institution's explanation of phenomena, and that is part and parcel of this present project. Magic appears to have what I call syntactical fluidity that depends on context, historical, literary, et cetera.

1.1 Language & Semantics: Signification and Ambiguity of Terms

It is difficult to assess an explanation of a belief, or a belief system in words, and harder still to assign signification to such inexplicable conviction[s]; however, as Saint Augustine (354-430 C.E.) has asserted in times past— *words are themselves signs*;[4] further, such attached signification tends to hold, I offer, subjective interpretations. For example, in utilizing the law of contraries[5] many dual subjects can be categorized and better understood in opposing classification; i.e. "hot and cold," "yeah or nay," "alpha and omega," "good and evil," and of course "black and white." Each pairing requires knowledge of the other's existence in order for the pair to reflect contrariety. Stuart Clark, in his massive study on witchcraft, *Thinking with Demons: the Idea of Witchcraft in Early Modern Europe* (herein, *Thinking*), suggests a motive for such prescriptive, dual classification. Clark posits that, "in the system of ideas that informed early Greek religion and natural philosophy, material flux and moral variety were traced to the interplay-sometimes the warring-of contrary entities in the

---

[4] This concept regarding words as signs is taken from Saint Augustine's *De Doctrina Christiana* (Books XIX-XXV), translated by R.P.H. Green, (Oxford University Press, 1997), p. 47-54.

[5] Isidore of Seville (c.560-April 6, 636) utilizes this concept, which develops from Aristotelian philosophy. Isidore accounts for such opposing binaries in his *Etymologiae*. The Latin text is edited as: *Etymologiarum siue originum libri xx*, ed. W.M. Lindsay, 2 vols. (1911. Oxford: Clarendon Press, 1957). There is now a complete English translation (including the relevant letters): *The Etymologies of Isidore of Seville*, trans. Stephen A. Barney et al. (Cambridge: Cambridge University Press, 2006). In his Latin text, "De Oppositis," Isidore asserts:

> Contrariorum genera quattuor sunt, quae Aristóteles ἀντικείμενα, id est opposita vocat, propter quod sibi velut ex adverso videntur obsistere, ut contraria; nec tamen omnia quae opponuntur sibi contraria sunt, sed omnia a contrario opposita sunt. (Lib. II xxxi; I5^v)

> There are four types of contraries (*contrarium*), which Aristotle calls ἀντικείμενα, that is 'opposites' (*oppositum*) because they seem to stand opposing one another as if face to face, as contraries. Still, not all things that are opposed (*opponere*) to one another are contraries, but all things are opposed by a contrary. (87-88)

Isidore's entire section regarding the subject of contraries can be found in the Latin, Lib. II xxxi; I 5v-I6v, or in the English translation; pages 87-88 respectively. Such ideation was representative in the medieval community in which Bishop Isidore had inherited from his brother, Bishop Leander of Seville, who had promoted Aristotelian ideals throughout his career, and which were catalogued for lasting effect in Isidore's aforementioned *Etymologiae*, the first medieval encyclopedia of its kind.

world" (*Thinking* 43). Clark continues to pay homage to such who held these views and their alternating [dis]ordering via the mention of Empedocles,[6] Pythagoras,[7] and of course Plato. In Plato (429-347 B.C.E.), Clark suggests that both the *Timaeus* and the *Symposium* are representations of "*concordia discors* in mathematical reasoning, musical harmony, physical health, moral improvement, and ultimately, the universal structure of things" (*Thinking* 43). These "things" could in fact provide clarification of the [un]seen world. Again, offering if nothing less an attempt at classifying magic as an explanation of phenomena.[8]

Specifically, Clark begins this elucidation by providing a Rhetoric of Witchcraft, or an attempt at language taxonomy regarding the ideation of witchcraft. It serves as perhaps an approach to the necessary disentanglement of the term *magic*. Clark begins by postulating "how language authorizes any kind of belief at all" (*Thinking* 3). What is more, this attempt is further problematized by the epiphenomenal impulses of other things; i.e. the explanation of phenomena is contextual and reflexive, wherein for one group it may symbolize ritual and religion versus for another assembly, distinct praxis and experimental science. Clark continues

---

[6] Empedocles (ca. 495-435 BCE), was a physician, philosopher, and to some extent a poet. His central work *On Nature* concerns us here because of his use of opposites and his roots, or four elements: fire, air, water and earth; each element is moved by two opposing forces, 'love' and 'strife,' respectively.

[7] Pythagoras (ca. 571-c.a. 496 BC), or as Carl Huffman states, "the man who knew many things," (*Stanford Encyclopedia of Philosophy* online) positions the philosopher as a mathematician and mystic. According to Diané Collinson in her *Fifty Major Philosophers* (New York: Routledge, 2002), Pythagoras concerns us in this project because, as Collinson suggests, "The Pythagorean study of number and its relationship with the physical universe, and especially its relationship with music and astronomy, produced a strange blend of mysticism and real mathematical development" (9). Further, Collinson refers to the astronomical tendencies that were applicable via a Pythagorean understanding of music and harmony amongst the stars. She asserts, "He [Pythagoras] thought that the heavens were like a musical scale, that the stars produced harmonies and that souls at their best must be harmonious with the heavens" (9).

[8] In utilizing the term phenomena I am adhering to the Oxford English Dictionary (OED) for its range of meanings; i.e. A thing which appears, or which is perceived or observed; a particular (kind of) fact, occurrence, or change as perceived through the senses or known intellectually; *esp.* a fact or occurrence, the cause or explanation of which is in question ("phenomena [-non]"). This definition applied to a definition of magic is the purpose of my overall study on the explanation of white and black magic-respectively; or, *miraculum* and *maleficium*.

his investigation of language engaging in the idea of inversion,[9] albeit another layering to this project's suggestion of contraries, and asserts, "Thus inversion can have an estranging as well as clarifying role; it unsettles the very classification system that gives it meaning and does so in the same instant that that meaning is grasped" (28). Arguably, such explanation of phenomena amidst inversion or contrariety assists in the explanatory role as well as adding to its imperceptibility. Perhaps then, the role of "magic" and its classification continues to be ambiguous even in contextual spaces. Arguably, magic aligned well and within the infrastructure that comprised both religion and science, respectively. Clark continues his investigation for a Rhetoric of witchcraft in terms of values and dual classification and contrariety. Moreover, in terms of the comprehension of ideas, "opposites were said to require each other in order to form wholes and improve understanding" (40). Clark recounts such logic as operative in modern Europe:

> In the primary opposition of good/evil, evil is needed as much as good. As the complement of good it complements the order of things; indeed, it makes the order perfect. The same must be true of demons and witches, who thus become both distillations of everything negative and, at the same time, vehicles of consummation. (41)

By Clark's account then, the application of each element within the binary "good" v. "evil" is both actively responsible for each other, and registers its complementarity. Moroever, such a bold contention is not new, as it was taken into account in early modern Europe wherever the Church desired authority. Clark terminates his section on language with the ideation of contrariety and its universal appeal. He asserts, "Contrariety was thus a universal principle of intelligibility as well as a statement about how the world was actually constituted," and again insists "this had implications for the way men and women used language" (54). Accordingly, this was not mere heuristic conventions at work, but as Clark suggests, "an imperative at

---

[9] Clark utilizes the term inversion with regards to contrariety and opposing binaries. He specifically engages with the role perception holds via the onlooker. Essentially, I take the term "perception" to function as a gaze upon context, and an examination given via language, or words attached with signification. Clark states, "Inversion too…was a feature of the world of sin, a world in which the negative qualities threatened to dominate their positive counterweights, and all things echoed the primal disobedience by reversing their normal roles and relationships" (*Thinking* 71). Clark assumes much here, with regard to such loaded terms such as *sin* and *normal*. Perhaps, this view of the world-turned-upside-down motif could in fact behave as a proviso to explanatory phenomena and other recognizable [dis]order.

work" (54). The shift from language to religion was not only inevitable in describing phenomena, but *natural* and pressing.

According to historian Richard Kieckhefer's *Magic in the Middle Ages* (herein, *Magic*), "some of the classic anthropological definitions assume that religion and magic stand in relationship of binary opposition […] religion is public and official while magic is private and unofficial" (x). Religion has a long and tumultuous history on its own and the formation of Christian doctrine[10] itself not an easy matter to settle into mere words; it is not, however, the scope of this project to provide a detailed account of Religion, but simply to suggest that it served as one of the binaries in question against which a definition of magic is sometimes proposed. Of course, there are those who suggest, like Jennifer M. Corry in her *Perceptions of Magic in Medieval Spanish Literature* (herein, *Perceptions*), that the Church retaliated with their own version of magic in the form of *white* magic, or the explanation of phenomena via *miraculum*. Herein, we begin to note that what is at stake is not necessarily the term "magic" per se, but the source of power and influence at which an explanation of the [un]known hinges; i.e. demonic magic is dark, "black" magic for its invocation of demonic power and "white" magic is its opposite, because its source of power stems from God and the agents of the Divine. Hence, the syntax of magic, albeit an arbitrary term, perhaps is not assigned a "good" or an "evil" connotation until the source of power or cause of influence is determinable.

Consequently, black magic, or as Kieckhefer has stated, *nigromancia* or the black arts, as it is aptly ascribed, utilizes the invocation of demons and blackened spirits.[11] The Church,[12] seen as the light bringers and bearers of

---

[10] For further reading concerning the subject of Church doctrine throughout history see Jaroslav Pelikan's *The Christian Tradition: A History of the Development of Doctrine*, 5 vols. (Chicago: University of Chicago Press, 1971-1991).

[11] Elsewhere and for further reading, Richard Kieckhefer has analyzed the role of "necromancy" in his *Forbidden Rites: A Necromancer's Manual from the Fifteenth Century* (University Park: Pennsylvania State University Press, 1998).

[12] By mention of the Church I am carefully considering the position of an Institution in direct opposition to Heresy and Paganism. It is under this direct contentious binary that magic can be considered. There are two distinct threads that can be discussed here. The first, involves the Church against Paganism, that is, Paganism as an institution that is considered as a rival to the position of the Church and its affectations for promoting its belief and belief systems. The second, concerns that of the Church order that opposed the use of magic as means to uncover the secrets of Nature. Why? Because coercion of Nature by [a] force that is construed as [un]natural is in direct contradiction to Divine power and Divine influence. Yet, as we shall note when clergymen dabbled in these "arts," distinctions of such practice[s] became considerably confused and ushered in the inevitable retaliation of Church

the good news, or the *godspel*, "good narrative" in Old English (which develops into modern English "gospel") stood in direct opposition to the black arts, and retaliated with explanations of their own regarding the supernatural. Though Kieckhefer maintains that such binary oppositions, in studying medieval culture, are not necessarily helpful,[13] I suggest that they may in fact provide some illumination with regards to how the participants in a medieval culture steeped in "magic" made sense of their everyday lives; i.e. through magic and its derivative forms and applications such as, conceivable explanations for crops going bad, the appearance of medical ailments and pestiferous, bodily growths, the onset of blindness and other maladies, and even looming, inclement weather patterns. It is this level of investment into the [un]known that could in fact provide the reasons to why people held specific beliefs and why, through the use of contraries were explanations not only foretold, but in some cases, as we shall see, demanded. Again, the wielders of such prescient arts were of some use to their respective culture[s], and could offer some indication of the medieval mind, and its direct affectation[s].

---

higher-ups to oversee and excise such behavior(s). Further, it suggests that magic could have very well been a part of religion and not necessarily outside of it; magic then, like other elements of theology, say angels and demons, is part of the world of Religion and from such binaries works towards an understanding of *miracula* versus *nigromancia*, or angels versus devils. Here, I am not so concerned with the historical residue of Church vs. Paganism, though it may indeed exist, as applied to an Iberian thirteenth century, but the position of magic couched in terms of religion and science, and its affectation via its practitioner's pre-witchcraze. Again, the relationship to be analyzed exists as magic and science as well as magic and religion. Still further, with regards to the term *institution* and the signification of "Paganism" and "Heresy" within these particular parameters a word or two may be in order.

The Church is an institution as to some extent "Paganism" may also be considered an institution. "Heresy" is an institution only when it becomes organized like "Islam," "Judaism," or "the Cathars." Otherwise, "Heresy" is the deviation of an individual from the teachings of the Church. This works only when "Heresy" and "Paganism" are capitalized and seen as "institution." The Church and the individual acts are not opposites. Individual acts are opposed to this as that element of Church teaching. But the Church prosecutes these individual acts vigorously as they may grow into an institution as happened as a consequence of Martin Luther's rejection of indulgences.

[13] Richard Kieckhefer in his seminal work *Magic in the Middle Ages* (Cambridge: Cambridge University Press, 2000), states: "I argued in this book that these binary oppositions are not helpful in studying medieval culture [...] and if we are to comprehend their (i.e. medieval clerics) culture it is important for us to know precisely how they supposed these practices worked" (xi). Kieckhefer suggests that the binary in question, religion and magic, are confusing set ups especially because these rational clerics would not confuse the two when explaining phenomena.

If opposites are indeed necessary for a more comprehensive explanation of one's world, rather than existing in isolation, what then were the distinct accountings involving the binary of black magic and white magic? For some perspective, Stuart Clark puts forward that "the important point is that, since contrariety was thought to categorize the logic of the Creator's own thinking, there was nothing to which it could not be applied…cosmological, ethical-social, and cognitive aspects" (*Thinking* 49). This application toward Church use is not a far stretch, but first, what of its dark counterpart?

In *Magic and the Middle Ages* (*Magic*) Richard Kieckhefer purports that "intellectuals in Medieval Europe recognized two forms of magic: natural and demonic" (9). These distinctions fall under the compartmentalization of science (early science at that) and *nigromancy* (necromancy, or learned magic arts).[14] Kieckhefer, like Stuart Clark before him, agrees that demonic magic was "not distinct from religion, but rather a perversion of religion" (9). Likewise, the former type of magic, or natural magic was not distinct from science itself, but was "a branch of science" (9). With such

---

[14] It should be noted that early on its inception 'necromancy' and 'nigromancy' were quite distinct. The first part of the word *necromancy* comes from the Greek νεμρός, "corpse," and involves calling up the dead or demons, and is a diabolical rather than a learned art. The first part of the word *nigromancy* is Latin, *niger*, "black," and while it may involve a pun on *necromancy*, it refers to the "Black Arts," and was in some circles taken as a positive term. In Book I, chapter III of the Latin *Picatrix*, it is described as follows: "Know that one calls this science nigromancy. We call nigromancy all that which a man brings about and at the end of which the intellect and the spirit are completely swept away by this process, and that with respect to the marvelous consequences by which one brings about that which the intellect observes through meditation and admiration." Béatrice Bakhouche et al., ed. *Picatrix: Un traité de magie medieval*. (Turnhout: Brepols, 2003), 47.

'Nigromancy' involves the learned, magic arts, and by the end of the Middle Ages these two terms were indeed conflated. Richard Kieckhefer in *Forbidden Rites: A Necromancer's Manual of the Fifteenth Century* (University Park, Pennsylvania: Pennsylvania State University Press, 1997) sheds some light with regards to both 'necromancy' and 'nigromancy' and he asserts:

> One might suggest the term *nigromantia* not be re-Graecized as 'necromancy' but left as 'nigromancy'. While in some respects preferable, this usage would mistakenly suggest that medieval usage distinguished between two terms. Both DuCange's *Glossarium* (s.v. *nigromantia*) and the *Oxford English Dictionary* (s.v. 'necromancy') make it clear that *nigromantia* was not a term distinct from *necromantia*, but an alternative version of the same word […] The equivalence thus conflated 'black divination' […] with 'divination by consulting the dead'. (19)

Nevertheless, the evidence from early Medieval Spain, especially, the *Picatrix*, suggests that in this time and place the two terms are distinguished.

"distinctions" in place the main problem involves defining magic altogether. In other words: *What exactly was it, and did it have a history*; or: *Was it part of the disentanglement of a larger belief system-religion and/or science.*[15] Arguably, as Bengt Ankarloo and Stuart Clark have stated in their six volume edited series, *Witchcraft and Magic in Europe*,[16] "European magic beliefs and actions...have a long prehistory" and again, that "the field is virtually open since all history has a prehistory without bounds" (I: xi). Hence, the ultimate inquiry is W*here exactly do we begin*, and W*hat are the reasons to do so*. The following is a survey of examples, or stories that detail the subject of both black and white magic and their derivative affectation as well as a survey of various dialogues involving the defining of the term *magic.*[17]

---

[15] Of course we must be careful with such modern words when applying them anachronistically to a distant historical period; i.e. we must be aware that religion and science may be contraries only from a modern point of view. As such a medieval monastic "scientist" may not have readily seen the distinction. Arguably, such ambiguities further lend themselves to the complex subject of "magic," which is easily encroached upon by and paired alongside with "religion" and "science" proper.
[16] Bengt Ankarloo and Stuart Clark, ed. *Witchcraft and Magic in Europe*, 6 vols. (Philadelphia: University of Pennsylvania Press, 1999-2002).
[17] Saint Augustine serves as a beginning point when defining the term *magic*. In his *De Doctrina Christiana*, Augustine argues that "there are two types of learning in a pagan society," and that furthermore, they exist via dual institutions, namely man[kind] and God (a position as we shall note later that Isidore of Seville supports in his *Etymologiae*). He purports:

> One consists of things which have been instituted by humans, the other consists of things already developed, or divinely instituted, which have been observed by them [i.e. the pagans]. Of those instituted by humans, some are superstitious, some not. (Book Two, XIX, p.47)

Concerning the subject of magic itself, Augustine rules against consultation with or contracts among false idols and the establishment of false worship of the creative order. Specifically, "Something instituted by humans is superstitious if it concerns the making and worshipping of idols [...] or if it involves certain kinds of consultations or contracts about meaning arranged and ratified with demons, such as the enterprises involved in the art of magic" (Book Two, XX, p. 48). Augustine's invective against the practice did not stop here, but contained a polemic stance with regards to mathematics and astrology within the context of prescient advising; i.e. the *art* of magic leads the people astray. Moreover, Augustine is concerned here with Paganism itself as an institution. In full he claims:

> We must not omit from this category of deadly superstition the people who are called *genthliaci* because of their study of natal days, or now in common parlance *mathematici* [astrologers]. Although they investigate the true position of the stars at a person's birth and sometimes actually succeed in

1.2 Black and White: Stories of Gray in Tales of Miracula and Maleficium

Jacob Bronowski enters the tête-à-tête of magic in his small volume, *Magic, Science, and Civilization* purporting that nature could be accessible via the right language. Bronowski further argues that it is best to do away with power-knowledge distinctions. He asserts, "above all you cannot make a distinction between power and knowledge, and that's a central distinction that magic makes" (20). Bronowski further disassociates science from magic altogether and to that effect asserts:

> I call everything magic which dualizes our view of the world [...] if you say "open sesame" then nature will open for you; if you are an expert then nature will open for you; [...] if you are an initiate there is some way of getting into nature which is not accessible to other people. (20)

---

working it out, the fact that they use it to try to predict our activities is a grave error and amounts to selling uneducated people into a wretched form of slavery. (Book Two, XX, p. 49)

The form of slavery in which Augustine makes reference to is submission to a preordained universe governed by the stars and allegiance to Mars or Venus rather than enjoying the freedom in a universe in which the individual has free will. Hence, in a final note, he urges, "So in all these teachings we must fear and avoid this alliance with demons, whose whole aim, in concert with their leader, the devil, is to cut off and obstruct our return to God" (Book Two, XXIII, p. 52). In short, Augustine equates any contract or connection with anything or anyone, outside the proper space of the Divine, via magic, as disruptive to the proper order or alliance which exists solely with God and not with devils. In another work Augustine directly challenges the belief of the Manicheans and sets up his counter-argument to the position of the term *magic* (*City of God*, Book X, Chapter 8 thru Chapter 12, herein expressed as X.8 followed by the respective page number).

Following Saint Augustine and his dialogues on the subject of magic, many added and attempted to define magic and its affectations. Such thinkers, though not an exhaustive list by any means, include Isidore De Seville (*Etymologiae*), Alfonso X (*Las Siete Partidas*), Robert Grosseteste (notions of creation *ex nihilo*), Roger Bacon (experiments as explanations of phenomena, specifically alchemy), Albertus Magnus (*De Anime in arte alchemiae*) and of course Saint Thomas Aquinas (*Summa Theologiae* and his commentary on Aristotle's *Metaphysics*). Consequently, such members of their particular medieval intelligentsia shaped, challenged, and provided ongoing discursive measures for the comprehension of the [un]known and the [un]seen through a rational lens, and it is not without import that this is part of the impulse that gave rise to the establishment of Universities throughout Europe.

His reasoning is as ambiguous as his analysis; he states, "The form of magic that I shall discuss is the notion that there is a way of having power over nature which simply depends on hitting the right key" (20). If nothing else then, this analysis may help to point us in a formative direction regarding a beginning concept of magic over nature; i.e. where the natural realm is subservient to the powers that affect it, whereby left to itself, nature may not so willingly yield to its *abuser*. Moreover, who were these vessels who held the *right* key, suggesting that otherwise nature herself was perhaps...locked? Bronowski cites as an example, a witch (typical wielder of the dark arts) riding her broomstick backwards, suggestive of an aberrant behavior altogether with what he considers magic to have "a tendency...to turn nature upside-down" (21). Still, Bronowski did have something to say concerning white magic as the antithetical position of black magic. He states, "yes, there is a magic, but it is a natural magic, a *white* magic...no one knows quite how it works, but it attempts to extract out of the universe its own harmonies for our good" (31). Undoubtedly, Bronowski is alluding to Pythagorean ideals regarding the subject of planetary alignments and their harmonious intention to work with and within nature, not subjugate it. This, Bronowski suggests, is a step toward sympathetic, if not, appreciative science "as we understand it" (31). Until now, recent scholarship has suggested magic in other terms like a model of sorts rather than as an actuality.

In volume three, *The Middle Ages* of the celebrated series, *Witchcraft and Magic in Europe* edited by Bengt Ankarloo and Stuart Clark, scholar Karen Louise Jolly argues, "magic is more of a concept rather than a reality," and that moreover, "the term is a way of categorizing a wide array of beliefs and practices, ranging from astrology and alchemy, charms and amulets, to sorcery and necromancy, trickery and entertainment, as practiced by both laity and clergy" (3:3). Jolly further argues that the label applied to phenomena via magic, science or religion was contextual; i.e. "certain practices in medieval Europe come to be labeled as magic, as opposed to scientific or religious, [and, it] depends on the perspective of the person using the label" (3:3). The focus of such a definition of magic carries with it Jolly's ideation of alterity. She suggests, "Magic is most often a label used to identify ideas or persons who fall outside the norms of society and are thereby marked as special or non-normative, either for the purpose of exclusion or to heighten a sense of mysterious power inherent in their status" (3:6). Jolly, like Kieckhefer and others agree that medieval thought on magic and science is based on rationality; i.e. magic came to be seen as unsystematic, manipulative and irrational while science was affirmative and rational in application.[18] However, in the early Middle Ages as the *Picatrix* demonstrates, *nigromancy* was seen as an integral part of what we now call science, and in some sense was regarded as the culmination of it.[19]

Jolly terminates her study by alluding to a paradigm shift regarding magic in the thirteenth century. She claims, "The official Church stance regarding magic shifted from a demonic association with paganism to a demonic association with heresy" (3:21). Arguably then, in the pre-thirteenth century when, the focus on the source of power, was seen to be demonic, "magic" was classified alongside Paganism because of its systematic threat to the Church. Hence, it is black magic that is spoken of here, and not white magic. To which she claims the former to be the dominant view, but the latter a conundrum of sorts. In her own words, "Why and how these forms [via the Church] of magic develop in this high medieval environment continues to be a puzzle" (3:23). Moreover, Jolly in her study, continues to look into the affectations of magic, such as: the uses of medical magic and the healing of the body and soul, ritual performance involving post-Augustinian notions of words and signs, the use of magic to ward off disease and natural disaster, acquired knowledge via astrology and divination from Nature, occult knowledge via sorcery and necromancy, and she even examines how magic can provide entertainment. In one example concerning the ambiguity of magic, Jolly cites Gregory of Tours (c. 538-c. 594) telling the story of St. Martin raising a tree that had fallen across the road by the signing of the cross. The people who witnessed such an event proceeded to scrape the very bark from off of the tree and dissolved its contents into some water to make a medicine. Apparently, such medicine could cure invisible ailments from "airborne poisons, elves, dwarves, or demons" (30). In some cases medical "magic" acting under the agency of medicine alleviated particular, sympathetic ailments; i.e. a popular example was the use of a vulture's liver to heal those with liver complaints. Further, with application of medical magic the three most common complaints, according to Jolly, were "worms, bleeding, and childbirth," (3:35) and these

---

[18] Such distinctions and pairings concerning magic and science or magic and religion are confusing, but it should be noted that magic too could be held in rational, learned circles as is suggested by the definition of *nigromancia* given earlier; and, what is more, "magic" could also be seen as supplicative in prayer, but note that such entreaty was directed toward the Devil and not toward a benevolent Creator.

[19] Jolly is generalizing about all of the Middle Ages (B.C.E. 750-1500) but privileging the latter centuries. Moreover, it is not a matter of "magic" being positioned with religion by clerical scholars who were engaged in research we would now call "magic." For such scholars, such a distinction did not exist as the *Picatrix* makes quite clear.

three disorders benefited from such medical practices. What is more, accounts of saints spitting on leaves and applying mud to affected areas alongside the signing of the cross, produced a belief in their healing powers. Even the grinding of special stones into a drink with the heads of snakes to ward off enemies (usually demons) could be utilized. With respect to the affectation of words spoken during such magical rituals, Jolly states: "The basis for the power of narration lies in a particular view of language, that words represent reality and their performance can therefore alter reality" (3:39).[20] Of further interest is the subject of magic as entertainment. Magic, as stated earlier held a position of entertainment,[21] a position that tested the mind of its audience (in the guise of deception), but in reality challenged "ideas and human relationships" (3:66). Seemingly, this entertainment was non-threatening and couched magic in the frame of illusion, minstrels, acrobats, and involved an aristocracy "fascinated with automatons" (3:67); moreover, magic in general was seen as *superstitio* and the lines of distinction between belief and itself were often blurred, regardless of its "soft," or subtle utility. Moreover, if magic and belief were in communion— could the same solution work in tandem with science; i.e. could magic prove soluble in the water of experimental science?

Roger Bacon (1214-1292), a thirteenth century friar residing in England gained notoriety posthumously, and was termed by many as a sorcerer. Why? His practice of alchemy, the early beginnings of scientific experimentation resulting in modern day Chemistry, positioned him as a heretic. Though a friar of the Order of St. Francis, he spent his waning years in prison for promoting dangerous and demonic ideas, and died one year after his release (a fate reminiscent of that suffered by Galileo, another man of science in conflict with the Church). Still, Bacon held himself to the

---

[20] See also, Karen Louis Jolly, *Popular Religion in Late Anglo Saxon England: Elf Charms in Context* (Chapel Hill: University of North Carolina Press, 1996). Of strong interest is her story concerning the surviving Old English charms which need to be spoken/performed for them to be effective (as opposed to phylacteries or talismans where the mere presence of the written word is sufficient to effect a result).

[21] I agree with Karen Jolly that magic as "entertainment" is a modern anachronism of sorts, and that such amusement often involved the space of the court. One example, posits the life of an astrologer, a master of arcane knowledge, who predicted the death of the woman whom the king (Louis XI, 1425-1483) had loved. The king, out of sorts, secretly prepared the death of this particular astrologer, and on the given day asked him to predict his own death. The clever astrologer responded by predicting his death three days before the death of the king, and as such the king was keen to keep this particular astrologer alive and well. A story, such as this one, reflects Jolly, "true or not, indicates the fragile balance between belief and doubt in the political context of magic" (68).

highest code of ethics when writing his works commissioned by Pope
Clement IV;[22] these works include the *Opus Maius*, the *Opus Minus* and the
Opus Tertium. In his *Opus Tertium*, Bacon writes, according to G.R. Evans'
Fifty Key Medieval Thinkers, "What is the purpose of study?" (118). To
which Evans suggests, "The *utilitas philosophiae*, the benefit or value of
philosophy, must, he [Bacon] believes, be to theology, in encouraging the
conversions of unbelievers" (118). Further, Bacon was such a staunch
supporter of the faith that he is recorded with stating the following, "children
should begin with the more straightforward books of Scripture [...] rather
than with such unedifying classical poets as Ovid" (118). Seemingly then,
such clear dictates in support of the faith should surely not involve a man of
the cloth alongside condemnation for heresy and incarceration. However,
Bacon did have the knack for science and his rhetoric oftentimes confused
the Church of his ultimate stance.[23] For example, when addressing the
subject of proofs and religion, Bacon asserts, "Arguments prove nothing
unless they are supported by the results of experiments" (Evans 119).
Further, such a claim seeks a balance that the Church was unwilling to settle
upon, and Bacon, according to G.R. Evans, suggestively "balances 'all the
works of experimental science (*scientia experimentalis*) and other wonders
(*mirabilia*)' carefully against magical arts" (120). Bacon provides a snapshot
of English thirteenth century ecclesiastical intolerance as well as the clergy's
invested position and interest in the practice of magic. More importantly,
Bacon affords yet another contribution to the entangled dialogue between
magic and science as well as between magic and religion. And due to the
fame that was acquired *post mortem*, Bacon's infamy was due more to
superstition and hearsay rather than any consideration of his written
materials.

In Part III of the *Witchcraft and Magic in Europe: the Middle Ages*,
Edward Peters in his first chapter, "Superstition and Magic from Augustine
to Isidore of Seville," opens with:

> Christian writers first encountered the Latin words *superstitio* and *magia*
> when Greek and Roman writers and rulers applied them to Christianity itself

---

[22] Pope Clement IV was born at Saint-Gilles on the Rhone, 23 November, year
unknown; he died in 1268.
[23] If by "stance" we can freely interchange such a term with "faith," that encapsulated
belief warranting thought and action in like vein to act via a higher standard, then
Bacon not only possessed the fullness of such a stance—it overflowed into
everything he accomplished and tackled, and yet the Church was not able to
understand nor comprehend Baconian interfaith. Truly, he was a man before his time,
and he was punished for it.

in their combined senses of divination, magic, secret and forbidden practices, and excessive religious fear. (178)

Peters' statement is an accounting of an early usage of the terms "superstition" and "magic," whereby those who wielded the terminology and regulated its signification ultimately gained; contrastingly, those who did not gain from such word privilege were often seen as other, and received a hegemonic labeling to reflect their alterity. Peters continues his point suggesting:

> Christians in turn reversed the usage: for them, superstition referred to what they considered to be the irrational and false beliefs—that is, the 'religions'—of all others besides Christians and, to a limited extent, Jews, although Christian scripture portrayed some Jews as magicians (Acts 13: 6-12; 19: 13-20) and the poisonous image of the Jew as sorcerer survived for a long time in later European thought. (178)

The use of "magic" here is polemical among Christians, Romans and any other religious group who might wish to malign their opponents; and Christians used it in their formation of an attitude toward heresy. Why? The stakes concerning the subject of magic were higher and the attack on it was inevitable. No longer was death, which took care of the corporeal entity, sufficient punishment. No, the spirit too had to be punished through anathema and excommunication, which it was believed consigned the spirit to eternal damnation.[24]

Saint Augustine (354-430 C.E.), championed and influenced a Christian reliance and understanding on the distinction between the black arts and true religion; between magic and sensation; and even between *miraculum* and *mira*, which concerned the subject of wonders. Here, Augustine provides initial insight into, what seemed to him a needless bifurcation of magic as learned magic, or theurgy[25] and low or fraudulent ritual. It did not matter.

---

[24] For an initial look into the inquisition and its uses of excommunication see Henry Charles Lea, *The Inquisition of the Middle Ages: Its Organization and Operation* (New York: The Citadel Press, 1954) [=chapters 7-14 of vol. 1 of Henry Charles Lea, *The Inquisition of the Middle Ages*, 3 vols. [New York: Harpers, 1887]).

[25] Augustine references magic and sorcery alongside the subject of theurgy. In Book X, Chapter 9 of *City of God* he asserts:

> They [miracles] were achieved by simple faith and devout confidence, not by spells and charms composed according to the rules of criminal superstition, the craft which is called magic, or sorcery—a name of detestation—or by the more honourable title of 'theurgy'. (383)

Magic, for Augustine, was an aberrancy altogether—regardless of the level of learning involved.[26]

Further, Augustinian thinking provided distinctions and definitions for miracles (*mirabilia*), and provided once more both an explanation and grounding toward the formation of Church doctrine. In Book X, Chapter 8 of *City of God*, Augustine makes his case for the use of miracles amidst the backdrop of the biblical story of Moses,[27] the prophet of God and the magicians of Pharaoh, King of Egypt. He states:

> The magicians achieved their effects by the use of enchantments and magical spells, the specialties of evil angels, that is, of demons; but Moses wielded a power that was as much greater as his cause more just, as he easily prevailed over them in the name God, the creator of heaven and earth, with the assistance of the angels. (Book X.8.382)

Augustine utilizes a pairing mechanism, suggestive of the law of contraries; i.e. he begins with the quasi-analogy: an evil angel is to demon and magic, as an angel is to God and a prevailing order. Moses is seen as the miracle worker, and such *mirabilia*, or "miracles and many others of the same kind [...] were intended to support the worship of the one true God," and once more—such devotion was to be "achieved by simple faith and devout confidence, not by spells and charms composed according to the

---

Further, Augustine posits that "theurgy: divination bringing man into contact with deity either by raising the visionary in an ecstasy, or by bringing down the divinity by means of magical arts" (X.9. p. 383). As pertaining to magic specifically, Augustine asserts: "Magic secured indirect revelation, in which the divinity appeared in some material object (e.g. a flame, in 'lychnomancy'), or through a medium in a trance" (384). What is more Augustine quotes the inconsistency of Porphyry asserting: On this evidence, as he [Porphyry] admits, theurgy is a science capable of achieving good or evil, whether among men or among gods" (385).

[26] This discussion regarding the learned distinctions and applications of 'high' and 'low' magic and its justification are taken up in Saint Augustine's works, most notably the colossal *City of God* and the shorter *De Doctrina Christiana*. I quote Edward Peters' description of the Augustinian position in full here:

> Augustine took up the problem of superstition and magic again in his massive work *City of God*, a vast meditation on human history and the ultimate purpose of human existence [...] In book X.9, Augustine dismisses the pretensions of learned pagans that theirs was a purer and higher art than lowly necromancy or everyday private consultation of magicians, identifying both 'high' and 'low' magic as 'engaged in the fraudulent rites of demons'.
> (183)

[27] See as a beginning point Exodus 7:10 and follow the development of magic and miracle in subsequent chapters in Exodus 8 through 11.

rules of criminal superstition, the craft which is called magic, or sorcery-a name of detestation" (Book X.9.383). Clearly, Augustine is not in favor of the dark arts nor its praxis, but what about the subject of miracles itself. We have suggested that such a term was still needed to explain phenomena, or events that occurred beyond the natural, even though it may have been more a matter of semantics rather than substance; such events were said to be *super*natural and concerned both *mirabilia* and *miracula*. Augustine further comments on the rhetoric applied to magic as well as the delusion of astrology and divination. For Augustine, the supporters of this magic do so "with the demons of delusion" (Book X.9.389), and yet "contrasted with these are all the miracles which are effected by divine power, whether by means of angels or […] the one God, in whom alone is the life of blessedness" (Book X.12.390). Once more we return to the axis point regarding what can be considered dark magic versus white magic, a distinction in which even Augustine's words prove supportive; i.e. it is a work or art through specific agency, or source of power. As a final thought concerning the subject of magic as it pertains to demons, Augustine posits the true role of God versus pseudo-divinity (ascribed to demon agency) as "they cannot be gods, or even good demons: they are either identical with that being who is called the Deceiver, or else they are nothing but a figment of the human imagination *and perhaps a passing memory* (Book X.13.389-90). Moreover, where Augustine provided a type of beginning point for Church examination concerning the explanation of phenomena, the extension of the subject continued without impairment, in the cataloguing works of Isidore of Seville.

1.3 Etymologiae: Bishop Isidore & the Classical
Value of a Pre-History

Isidore of Seville (c.560-April 6, 636),[28] in his encyclopedic *Etymologiae* attacks the subject of magic and superstition, but in the context, according to Edward Peters, of religious, synoptical preservation regarding "laws, rules and ecclesiastical legislation" (185). Hence, a definition of magic now enters into the realm of juridical and political discourse. Though Isidore contested Heresy and the schism between the Christians and the Jews, Pagan culture and practices, and comments on the subject of the *magi* with regards to his commentary on the story of Moses and Pharaoh's magician, we are concerned here in particular with his views on astrology, a practice intertwined with the subject of magic that was held to portray, through divination, a revelation of sorts to understanding the future. But first, what kind of man (of God) was Isidore of Seville exactly? Perhaps, a look into his epistolary writings will provide not only a sketch of such an individual, but may even afford a forecast of the climate of Spain during this time period.

The Letters of St. Isidore of Seville (herein, *Letters*), translated from the Latin by Gordon B. Ford, and more recently by Stephen A. Barney et al.,[29] are representative of the great man's heart and ethic in his striving for a good life, a *vita* steeped in the *veritas* of God and his people. As we shall note, Isidore received, what could be construed as ecclesiastical admonishment,

---

[28] In Joseph F. O'Callaghan's *A History of Medieval Spain* (herein, *A History*), the character of Isidore of Seville is first approached through the shadow of his brother, Saint Leander, bishop of Seville (c. 578-599). By O'Callaghan's accounts Saint Leander "was one of the most influential figures of the century" (*A History* 85). His main contribution concerned the preparation of a space for educating the mind and living the application of sound learning *bonus fides*. O'Callaghan suggests that:
> By organizing a school at Seville for the training of the clergy and by building up a library of the best pagan and Christian authors, Leander prepared the way for the fruitful labors of his brother, St. Isidore, who paid this tribute to him.
It was Leander who educated and trained his brother, and "though not a creative genius," Isidore "was a man of great learning and broad intellectual interests with great enthusiasm for the wisdom of the past" (*A History* 85). Clearly, such were the tools necessary for his impressive work, the *Etymologiae*.
[29] The English translation of the *Epistolae* is taken from Stephen A. Barney et al. Further, it should be noted that, according to the translators, these letters of correspondence, though not all of them, precede the *Etymologiae* in the early manuscripts. I have utilized the G. B. Ford Jr. translation, *The Letters of St. Isidore of Seville* (*Letters*), second ed. (Amsterdam: Hakkert, 1970) only where Stephen A. Barney et al. has not supplied the letters in question.

from Bishop Braulio, for receiving (from God) the gift of high intelligence and intellect, and not sharing such an encyclopedic mind quickly enough with his peers.[30] In *Epistolae* II, written around c.610-620, "Isidore to Archdeacon Braulio," Isidore begins in the Pauline epistolary form; i.e. he opens with "In christo charissimo, et dilectissimo filio, Braulioni archidiacono, Isidorus," ["From Isidore to my lord and most beloved son in Christ, Archdeacon Braulio"] (*Sancti Isidori Epistolae*, Epistolae II.18, *Correspondence of Isidore and Braulio*, A., p. 409) and continues to itemize his friendship via the symbolism of amity in both a ring and a cloak (*Letters* 19). He even justifies the purpose of the epistolary form stating, "Direximus tibi annulum propter nostrum animum, et pallium pro amicitiarum nostrarum amictu, unde antiquitas hoc traxit vocabulum," ["I have dispatched a ring to you on account of my affection, and also a mantle for a cloak (*amictus*) of my friendship (*amicitia*), whence this word was drawn in antiquity"] (*Epistolae* II.18, *Correspondence* A., p. 409). We find Isidore, the educator, under the motive of edification. In *Epistolae* III Isidore humbly submits a book of synonyms to his dear friend Archdeacon Braulio "non pro id quod alcijus utilitatis sit, sed quia eum volueras," [not because it is of some utility, but because you wanted it"] (*Epistola*e III.20, Correspondence B., p. 409). His relationship with Braulio suggests such an intimacy that Isidore was not afraid to state his weaknesses or to correct such inefficacy in others. In *Epistolae* VI to General Claudius, Isidore opens in his usual manner with, "Dilecto in Christo filio Claudio duci Isidorus," ["Isidore to General Claudius, beloved son in Christ"] (*Epistolae* VI.30, G. B. Ford's English trans., *Letter VI.*, p. 31) and proceeds to address what questions General Claudius had concerning the "Catholic faith" (Ford 31). His reason—to deter even those in power from heretical ideology. Elsewhere, Isidore continues this thought with regards to the heretical, especially towards those who are outwardly sheep, but inwardly wolves of deceit contesting that, "if (may it not be so) he is not manifestly unfaithful, our obedience is harmed in no way unless he teaches against the faith" (Ford 31).[31] As stated earlier, at

---

[30] The discussion concerning the subject of intelligence versus intellect, and the wedding and divorcing of the two can be followed in the seminal work by Jacques Barzun, *The House of Intellect* (New York: Harper & Row, 1961). Essentially, we are born with intelligence, but gather intellect; the former cannot be helped and the latter can be conceived as supplemental to it.

[31] This specific point of teachers spoiling the faith of many can be noted in Isidore's assertion about prelates who are also corrupt. He states that "Bad prelates should also be obeyed in doubtful orders as long as the Church tolerates them unless a suspicion of heresy can justly result from the prelate's manifest defamation in his teaching" (*Letters* 31). Suggestively, the stakes during such a time were high and *anathema*,

times the good Bishop Isidore had to be reminded of his promises and that
his *gift* for recording and itemizing and explaining the things of God was
from the Divine, and not to be kept for his own use.

In *Epistolae* X: Bishop Braulio to Isidore, Braulio opens his epistle with
a similar rhetorical approach that is congruent to the Isidoran letters. He
states, "Domno meo et vere domino Christique electo Isidoro Episcoporum
summo Braulio servus inutilis sanctorum Dei," ["Braulio, the useless servant
of the saints of God, to my lord and indeed master, Isidore, highest of
bishops, chosen of Christ"] (*Etymologiae* I, B2^v; p. 409). In his address to
Isidore he entreats the Bishop for the work that is to become the first
recorded encyclopedia in Western Civilization, Isidore's *Etymologiae*. We
pick up the quote in full as Braulio pleads:

> Suggereo   sane,   et   omnimoda   supplicatione   deposco,   ut   librum
> Etymologiarum, quem iam, favente Domino audivimus consummatum,
> promissionis vestræ memores, servo vestro dirigere iubeatis, quia, ut mihi
> conscius sum, magna ibi ex parte servi tui postulatione sudasti. (*Etymologiae*
> B2^v)

> I propose, indeed, and I request with every sort of entreaty that you,
> remembering your promise, will order that the book of *Etymologies* be sent
> to your servant, as we have heard that, God willing, it has been finished. As I
> am aware, you have sweated over it in large measure at the request of your
> servant. (Letter II, 410)

It seems that Bishop Braulio in this case may have been either an
impatient man, or Isidore was quite a busy one, unable to fulfill the "book
orders" of friends. Again, we find Bishop Braulio in complaint against
Isidore for the same work, the books of *Originum*, or *Origines*
(*Etymologiae*). In recounting such stories gathered from the *Epistolae*, or
Letters of Saint Isidore the purpose has been to add humanity and perhaps a
bit of mirth to an otherwise learned, meticulous and ambitious man of God.
We now move to a select discussion of Isidore's famous work in twenty
books, the *Etymologiae*.

The *Etymologiae* of Saint Isidore is quite simply a magnificent attempt at
what medieval historian Joseph F. O'Callaghan posits as, "the first of the
medieval encyclopedias. In twenty books he set out to summarize for the
benefit of future generations the learning of the ancient world" (*A History*
86). Further, O'Callaghan dissects Isidore's impressive text describing:

---

wherein the fulfillment of the warning found in the Epistles to the Galatians by the
Apostle Paul, was seriously considered (Galatians 1:9).

The breadth of the work is indicated by the table of contents; after treating the seven liberal arts, medicine, and jurisprudence, he turned to God, the angels, man, the state; the remaining books discuss such a variety of subjects as human anatomy, animals, cosmology, geography, minerals, metals, coins, weights, measures, agriculture, war, architecture, clothing, food, drink, and tools. (86)

Isidore's vast and wide-interest, plus high, mental acuity complemented his sagacious spirit. Still, what were some of the precepts to which he applied his prodigious, mental faculty? The following selections are brief in nature, but point the way into the expansive genius that was applied by Isidore of Seville.[32]

As mentioned earlier by the historian Joseph O'Callaghan, Isidore of Seville's *Etymologiae* begins with the discussion points concerning the *trivium* and quickly moves on to rhetoric and the dialectic, mathematics and medicine, and even commentary from the ancients concerning laws (jurisprudence) and the times. These ideas cover the first five books and book eight of the twenty books that comprise the *Etymologiae* and are listed as: *De Grammatica, De Rhetorica et Dialectica,* De Mathematica, *De Medicina,* and *De Legibus et Temporibvs, De Ecclesia et Sectis* or Book I. "Grammar," Book II. "Rhetoric and dialectic," Book III. "Mathematics," Book IV. "Medicine," Book V. "Laws and times," and Book VIII. "The Church and sects." It is not my intention to list out all of what Isidore set out to accomplish even in these six books, but to provide a survey of sorts outlining his sagacious mind and his polemic tendencies as well as his ability to inform and educate. In short, the *Etymologiae* existed to edify the Church and to set straight its detractors.

In the first book, *De Grammatica* (Grammar), Isidore is concerned with the subject of *ars*, or art and its Platonic and Aristotelian influences. Isidore asserts:

Ars vero dicta est, quod artis praeceptis regulisque consistat. Alii dicunt a Graecis hoc tractum esse vocabulum ἀπό τῆς ἀρετῆς, id est a virtute, quam scientiam vocaverunt. Inter artem et disciplinam Plato et Aristoteles hanc differentiam esse voluerunt, dicentes artem esse in his quae se et aliter habere possunt; disciplina vero est, quae de his agit quae aliter evenire non possunt. Nam quando veris disputationibus aliquid disseritur, disciplina erit: quando aliquid verisimile atque opinabile tractatur, nomen artis habebit. (I.i, C5ʳ)

---

[32] These selections are taken from Isidore's *Etymologiae* and include the first five books as well as Book Eight. For the English translation I have again relied on the Stephen A. Barney et al. translation (Cambridge: Cambridge University Press, 2006).

And an art (*ars*, gen.*artis*) is so called because it consists of strict (*artus*) precepts and rules. Others say this word is derived by the Greeks from the word ἀρετή, that is, 'virtue,' as they termed knowledge. Plato and Aristotle would speak of this distinction between an art and a discipline: an art consists of matters that can turn out in different ways, while a discipline is concerned with things that have only one possible outcome. Thus, when something is expounded with true arguments, it will be a discipline; when something merely resembling the truth and based on opinion is treated, it will have the name of an art. (Book I.i, 39)

Clearly, Isidore is interested in the ancient knowledge of art and imagery as well as in the methodology of classification. In the second chapter to this first book titled, *De Septem Liberalibvs Disciplinis*, ["The Seven Liberal Disciplines"] (I.ii, C5^r, Book I.ii, 39) Isidore lays claim to a prescriptive cataloguing of all seven criteria of the liberal arts, and continues his methodical list involving language and letters by citing along the way chapters within *De Grammatica* proper the following: *De Litteris Commvnibvs* ("The Common Letters of the alphabet"), *De litteris latinis* ("The Latin letters"), *De Grammatica* ("Grammar"), *De Partibvs Orationis* ("The parts of speech"), *De Nomine* ("The noun") and other parts of speech and language convention. Isidore challenges the reader in his *Etymologiae* to not lose sight of his central focus, namely edification and learning via a sound ethic. Before we depart the first book, the good Bishop in *De Differentiis*, or "Differentiation" (Chapter 31) argues for the position of *differentia*, or difference, and that which pertains to the design of difference. His main claim here and relevance for this overall project suggests that classification or naming exists in binaries, and that such opposing dual classification assists the other in its terminology and comprehension; essentially then, both are needed to make sense of the other's nomenclature. Specifically, Isidore asserts:

> Differentia est species definitionis, quam scriptores atrium de eodem et de altero nominant. Haec enim duo quadam inter se communione confusa, coniecta differentia secernuntur, per quam quid sit utrumque cognoscitur; ut cum quaeritur quid inter regem sit et tyrannum, adiecta differentia, quid uterque sit definitur, ut 'rex modestus est temperatus, tyrannus vero crudelis.' Inter haec enim duo differentia cum posita fuerit, quid sit utrumque cognoscitur. Sic et cetera. (I.xxxi, E5^v-E6^r)

> A differentiation (*differentia*) is a type of a definition, which writers on the liberal arts call 'concerning the same and the different.' Thus two things, of the kind that are confused with each other because of a certain quality that they have in common, are distinguished by an inferred difference, through which it is understood what each of the two is. For instance, one asks what is

the difference between a 'king' and a 'tyrant': we define what each is by applying a differentiation, so that "a king is restrained and temperate, but a tyrant is cruel." Thus when the differentiation between these two has been given, then one knows what each of them is. And so on in the same way. (I.xxxi, 55)

Recall then that, magic too is indeed ambiguous and imperceptible until we come across the source or influence of its power, thereby bifurcating dark or "black" magic against "white" magic or *miracula*; though distinct in name, both counter balance each other and register a stronger comprehension or value to their otherwise, isolated existence.

In the second and third books, *De Rhetorica et Dialectica* and *De Mathematica,* Isidore is concerned with Aristotelian *syllogismus*, as well as a definition for *genera causarum*, or the "kinds of arguments," *De Definitione Philosophiae*, the "definition of Philosophy" and *De Oppositis*, or "opposites." On this latter subject regarding opposites or contraries Isidore posits the customary four elements involving contrariety. He states:

Contrariorum genera quattuor sunt, quae Aristóteles ἀντικείμενα, id est opposita vocat, propter quod sibi velut ex adverso videntur obsistere, ut contraria; nec tamen omnia quae opponuntur sibi contraria sunt, sed omnia a contrario opposita sunt. (II.xxxi, I5ᵛ)

There are four types of contraries (*contrarium*), which Aristotle calls ἀντικείμενόν, that is, 'opposites' (*oppositum*) because they seem to stand opposing one another as if face to face, as contraries. Still, not all things that are opposed (*opponere*) to one another are contraries, but all things are opposed by a contrary. (II.xxxi, p. 87-88)

In his pontifical way Isidore continues to draw out the ideation of contrariety citing Cicero as calling the first contrary element *diversus*, or "diverse" followed by *relativus*, or "relatives," *habitus*, or "possession" as *orbatio* "lack," and termed by Cicero as 'privation' (*privatio*) and lastly, the fourth type of contrary "sets up an opposition 'from an affirmation and a negation' (*ex confirmatione et negatione*)," (II.xxxi, 88). In his third book, *De Mathematica* ("Mathematics"), Isidore gives a definition concerning the applied science of Astronomy. Under the section heading, *De Astronomiae,* ("Astronomy") we find a definition followed by chapter titles such as: *De Inventoribus, De Institutoribus eius, De Differentia Astronomiae et Astrologiae* and even *De Forma Mundi*, ["The Inventors of Astronomy," "Those who established Astronomy," "The difference between Astronomy and Astrology," and the "formation of the World"]. In brief, Isidore by definition suggests:

Astronomia est astrorum lex, quae cursus siderum et figuras et habitudenes stellarum circa se et circa terram indagabili ratione percurrit. (III.xxiv, L2^r)

Astronomy (*astronomia*) is the law...of the stars (*aster*), which, by investigative reasoning, touches on the courses of the constellations, and the figures and positions of the stars relative to each other and to the earth. (III.xxiv, 99)

Moreover, it was easy to note that via the ancients Isidore was equipping those who would come after him with the knowledge of such a study and application of the sciences. Still, Isidore was keen to not allow heresy and improper applications of such an art, to receive misrepresentation in any way. After all there was a difference between admiring the stars for their sake, and having them serve another person altogether that was counter-*naturalis*.

In his section xxvii, *De Differentia Astronomiae et Astrologiae* ("The differences between Astronomy and Astrology"), Isidore suggested that the distinction between the two studies is the motive of influence and the gathering of data that can then be put toward misuse, or toward the pursuit of power. He asserts:

Inter Astronomiam autem et Astrologiam aliquid differt. Nam Astronomia caeli conversionem, ortus, obitus motusque siderum continet, vel qua ex causa ita vocentur. Astrología vero partim naturalis, partim superstitiosa est. (III.xxvii, L2^v)

There is some difference between astronomy and astrology. Astronomy concerns itself with the turning of the heavens, the rising, setting, and motion of the stars, and where the constellations got their names. But astrology is partly natural, and partly superstitious. (III.xxvii, 99)

Again, here we note Isidore's care for recognizing distinctions and the reasons behind them that could potentially lead to more than mere ignorance.

In the fourth book, *De Medicina*, ["Medicine"], Isidore begins by defining health. He claims, "Sanitas est integritas corporis et temperantia naturae ex calido et humido, quod est sanguis; unde et sanitas dicta est, quasi sanguinis status," ["Health is integrity of the body and a balance of its nature with respect to its heat and moisture, which is its blood-hence health (*sanitas*) is so called, as if it were the condition of the blood (*sanguis*)"] (IV.v, M3^v; IV.v, 109). Isidore was well aware of the humors and the influence of simple "hot" or "cold" elements. He wrote extensively on the causes of ailments and where these ailments received their particular nomenclature; i.e. *febris* ("fever"), *lethargia* ("lethargy"), *inguen* ("swellings"), *lues* ("plague"), *epilemsia* ("epilepsy"), *melancholia* ("melancholy") and *typus* ("a cold fever"). He continues the chapter seemingly leaving no medical ailment that harms within and without the body; he covers such topics as hair loss, or *alopecia* (an ailment by which many suffer from today, present author included), diarrhea, paralysis, and even psychosis or maniacal behavior which he calls craziness or insanity. Thankfully, medicine is two-fold, and that which ails the body is expected to remedy itself, wherein homeostasis is not only achieved but desired and upon arrival, dearly welcomed. How better could Isidore reflect his community and offer proactive measures regarding medical taxonomy, if not by the book in which the articulation of the ancients were set down on vellum. In looking at *sanitas*, or "health"—Isidore's commentary on what exactly the term cure may have meant during the Antiquity and in the Middle Ages is formidable.

The fifth book, *De Legibus et Temporibus*, ("Laws and Times"), concerns important relevant positions for this project; i.e. we are here concerned with the natural laws that govern man and are set in motion via the Divine, and what constitutes a law as natural. Isidore pays homage to Moses and begins with his accounting of the laws of God to a people of God. He states, "Moyses gentis Hebraicae primus omnium divinas leges sacris litteris explicavit," ["Moses of the Hebrew people was the first of all to explain the divine laws, in the Sacred Scriptures"] (V.i, N3^r; V.i, 117). Further, all laws are construed of this bifurcation: human or Divine. Isidore asserts:

> Omnes autem leges aut divinae sunt, aut humanae. Divinae natura, humanae moribus constant; ideoque haec discrepant, quoniam aliae aliis gentibus placent. Fas lex divina est, ius lex humana. Transire per alienum fas est, ius non est. (V.ii, N3^v)

> All laws are either divine or human. Divine laws are based on nature, human law on customs. For this reason human laws may disagree, because different laws suit different peoples. *Fas* is divine law; jurisprudence (*ius*) is human law. To cross through a stranger's property is allowed by divine law; it is not allowed by human law. (V.ii, 117)

Suggestively, Isidore is making the parallel claim between natural law(s) adhering to a Divine presence that is stable and immutable and human law(s) which, in turn, is at best mimetic, but not transcendent. Isidore comments that such claims to human law, are fickle, and pass from person to person with some keeping, removing, and adding to the particular custom in question. Still, he does admit that law, is established via the people. Moreover, Isidore is concerned with reform and learned reform at that;

admittedly, he is of the ethic that if it is not fit on Earth, then it will not be fit for Heaven. Bishop Isidore sets out in this section of his *Etymologiae* a proviso of the law and what to do with those who are an aberrancy to society, a detriment to the masses (the Church and its faithful), and of course the inevitable explanation of the criminal is established. Specifically, Isidore was "careful" to semantically position the term sin alongside crime and law. For example, a couple of the titles of his chapters in *De Legibus et Temporibus* ("Laws and Times"), suggest *crimen* ("crime"), *facinus* ("misdeed"), and *malum* ("harm").

At the onset of this chapter I began by suggesting the Augustinian conception of signification via words, and that such classification of systems that interpret complex belief and belief systems is not only subjective, but as we have thus seen are at times imperceptible and simply problematic. This trend continues with the good Bishop of Seville. Isidore terminates this section of his fifth book discussing the terms *chronica*, or "succession of times," then *momenti et horae*, "moments and hours," *dies*, or "days" and of course *nox*, or "the night" and the *hebdomada*, or "week" as well as *de descriptione temporum*, or "a description of historical periods." The function of the world and the manner in which its inhabitants are to live concerned Isidore of Seville and none had a higher claim to positioning an informed Medieval Culture than the Bishop of Seville. Skipping over Book VI, *De Libris et Officiis Ecclesiasticus*, "Books and ecclesiastical offices,) and Book VII, *De Deo, Angelis et Sanctis*, "Of God, Angels, and Saints," we turn now to Book VIII, *De Ecclesia et Sectis*, or "The Church and Sects."

In Book VIII of the *Etymologiae* Isidore sets out to prescriptively explain the position of the Church, its structure and order, and affectations. Further, those elements which challenged Church hierarchy and its overall structure were also described and clearly marked as warnings by Isidore. In Chapter iii of Book VIII, *De Haeresi et Schismate* ("Heresy and schism"), Isidore opens with the subject of Heresy which is defined as choosing or choice. He states:

> Haeresis Graece ab electione vocatur, quod scilicet unusquisque id sibi eligat quod melius illi esse videtur, ut philosophi Peripatetici, Academici, et Epicurei et Stoici, vel sicut alii qui perversum dogma cogitantes arbitrio suo de Ecclesia recesserunt. (VIII.iii, X1^v)

> Heresy (*haeresis*) is so called in Greek from 'choice'…doubtless because each person chooses (*eligere*) for himself that which seems best to him, as did the Peripatetic, Academic, Epicurean, and Stoic philosophers-or just as others who, pondering perverse teachings, have withdrawn from the Church by their own will. (VIII.iii, 174)

Isidore goes on to define a *secta*, or "sect" and determines that it receives its name from *sequi*, or from following a pattern of belief (VIII.iii, 174). Combined, heresy and sect are two terms in which receive much attention and example as Isidore continues his chapters under such titles as: *De haeresibus Iudaeorum* ("Heresies of the Jews"), *De Haeresibus Christianorum* ("Christian Heresies"), *De Philosophis Gentium* ("Pagan Philosophers"), and of course *De Magis*, ("Magicians"). Isidore in identifying the *magi*, begins with Zoroaster, the first practitioner of the art. We pay particular attention to the source or coercion of influence via evil angels. He states:

> Itaque haec vanitas magicarum artium ex traditione angelorum malorum in toto terrarum orbe plurimis saeculis valuit. Per quandam scientiam futurorum et infernorum et vocationes eorum inventa sunt aruspicia, augurationes, et ipsa quae dicuntur oracula et necromantia. (VIII.ix, Y2^r)

> Consequently, this foolery of the magic arts held sway over the entire world for many centuries through the instruction of the evil angels. By a certain knowledge of things to come and of things below, and by invoking them, divinations (*aruspicium*) were invented, and auguries (*auguratio*), and those things that are called oracles (oraculum) and necromancy (*necromantium*). (VIII.ix., 181)

It is clear that Isidore finds such measures revolving around magic as 'foolish' and its practitioners of a likened disposition and constitution. Again, Isidore gives the reader his appreciation for knowledge, but its application toward an informed culture took precedence. In this case, the edification of the Church and its call to uphold a quality of life, albeit worthy to bare the name *holy*, was at stake; and where alliance to the enemies of the Church persisted—a compromised institution and its praxis was seen as problematic as well as its demise, inevitable. Further, Isidore is clever enough to position magic not only as foolish, but steeped in trickery. In suggesting the magicians of Pharaoh were tricksters he does not dispel their power, but cautions against their efficacy. He cautions:

> Nec mirum de magorum praestigiis, quorum in tantum prodiere maleficiorum artes ut etiam Moysi simillimis signis resisterent, vertentes virgas in dracones, aguas in sanguinem. (VIII.ix, Y2^r)

> There is nothing surprising about the trickery of the magicians, since their skills in magic advanced to such a point that they even countered Moses with very similar signs, turning staffs into serpents and water into blood. (VIII.ix, 181)

These magicians were powerful representations of an influence outside of Divine benevolence, or what C. Grant Loomis termed, *beneficium*, and acted in a manner more suitable to its opposite term, *maleficium*. Isidore continues to comment on the *maleficus*, or 'evil doers' as he posits:

> Magi sunt, qui vulgo malefici ob facinorum magnitudinem nuncupantur. Hi et elementa concutiunt, turbant mentes hominum, ac sine ullo veneni hausta violentia…interimunt. (VIII.ix, Y2^v)

> Daemonibus enim adcitis audent ventilare, ut quisque suos perimat malis artibus inimicos. Hi etiam sanguine utuntur et victimis, et saepe contingunt corpora mortuorum. Necromantii sunt quorum praecontationibus vidantur resuscitati mortui divinare, et ad interrogate respondere. (VIII.ix, Y2^v)

> There are magicians who are commonly called 'evildoers' (*maleficus*) by the crowd because of the magnitude of their crimes. They agitate the elements, disturb the minds of people, and slay without any drinking of poison, using the violence of spells alone. (VIII.ix, 182)

> With their summoning of demons, they dare to flaunt how one may slay his enemies with evil arts. They make use of blood and victims, and often handle the bodies of the dead. Necromancers (*necromantius*) are those by whose incantations the dead, brought back to life, seem to prophecy and to answer what is asked for… (VIII.ix, 182)

Evidently, such *agents* were assigned as evil doers and community leaders were made aware of such aberrant behavior[s] and practice[s]. Still, what can be said of the *necromantius*, or necromancer,[33] *hydromantius*, or hydromancer as well as other aspects of divination that utilized Christian ritual such as prayer and supplication; the referent here is to *Ariolo*, or *ara idolorum*, altar worshippers of idols. Isidore catalogued and placed each aberrant practice and derivative concerning the black art, or black magic as warnings toward a disruption in the Church. Arguably, one of his greater commentaries involves the astrological signs and the telling of the future via the stars and other celestial bodies. We begin with his commentary on the *astrologus*:

---

[33] It should be noted that the term necromancer along with astrology and astronomy have retained a currency down to the present while the other terms mentioned by Isidore have become obscure. Further, while necromancy was always a negative term, the related term nigromancy, as we have already noted, in which the first element is "niger," or "black," appears to be a pun on necromancy, but meaning the "black arts" and at least in some circles a positive term—although the two terms became synonymous.

Astrologi dicti, eo quod in astris auguriantur. Genethliaci appellati propter natalium considerationes dierum. Geneses enim hominum per duodecim caeli signa describunt, siderumque cursu nascentium mores, actus, eventa praedicare conantur, id est, quis quale signo fuerit natus, aut quem effectum habeat vitae que nascitur. (VIII.ix, Y3^{v-r})

Astrologers (*astrologus*) are so called, because they perform augury from the stars. *Genethliaci* are so called on account of their examinations of nativities, for they describe the nativities (*genesis*) of people according to the twelve signs of the heavens, and attempt to predict the characters, actions, and circumstances of people by the course of the stars at their birth, that is, who was born under what star, or what outcome of life the person who is born would have. (VIII.ix, 182)

The conventions of Astronomy, Astrology and the uses of the zodiac sign alongside the reading of the horoscope and the astrolabe, are outside the scope of this thesis. What is important here, however, is the sense in how Isidore understood the use of information and how he related to it from the ancient past. Recall, as he is writing his *Etymologiae* entry after entry, he is in sole control of his intention, which was to edify the Church and provide his community with an awareness of information from the Aristotelian past. He continues in this like vein regarding Astrology and its celestial interpretive "powers" ultimately engaging with the *magus*, or what Isidore terms "Primum autem idem stellarum interpretes magi nuncupabantur," ["the first interpreters of the stars were called Magi (*magus*)"] (VIII.ix, Y3^{v}; VIII.ix, 183).[34] Isidore concludes book VIII of his *Etymologiae* looking into the role of pagans and pagan gods and how dæmons were nothing more than *praevaricatores angeli, quorum Diabolus princeps est* (VIII.xi, Y5^{v}); "prevaricator angels, of whom the Devil is the ruler" (VIII.xi, 184). Again, such harsh attacks on the subject of magic and its affectation, though hostile, were representative of a contentious period and perhaps even a barometric fear of the inexplicable. Such uses of divination relied on the source, *Satanas*, or the adversary of God and of mankind, and Isidore wrote extensively on this subject for the ultimate purpose-to inform and preserve a knowing of the past that may indeed prove helpful toward a future Spain. Moreover, it was because of such literary documentation that we can receive

---

[34] Isidore notes such Magi are encountered in the gospel narrative of Christ's birth and adds: "Cuius artis scientia usque ad Evangelium fuit concessa, ut Christo edito nemo exinde natiuvtatem alicuius de caelo interpretaretur" (VIII.ix,Y3^{v}) ["Knowledge of this skill was permitted only up until the time of the Gospels, so that once Christ was born no one thereafter would interpret the birth of anyone from the heavens" (VIII.ix.183]).

an idea as to what information was readily available to the literate classes during the seventh century up through the thirteenth century. After all the Church relied on the accounts of Bishop Isidore of Seville as well as others who benefited from his reverberating *alarm*.

We began this rather entangled listing of magic and its derivatives with the idea that magic itself is somewhat ambiguous and reflective of a symbolism steeped in the bifurcation of terms. It seems that the source of power has influence as to what adjective modifies the term *magic*; i.e. demonic power utilizes and is responsible for dark, "black" magic and divine power utilizes and is responsible for "white" magic. Perhaps, a few words are in order for discussion of the latter term here; i.e. a brief continuation of sorts regarding the term "white" magic. We pick up the dialogue at a later time than the thirteenth century because, where I have looked, no philosopher was concerned with the position of miracles and its affectation on other belief and belief systems, in accordance to this project regarding magic and its ambiguous practice.[35] This is not a full digression, but a needful layering into the complexity of the overall term *magic*. Following such a brief look into "white" magic, we will then return to some further accounts involving magic and its affectations.

---

[35] In looking forward regarding the subject of "white" magic I would be remised if I did not acknowledge the contribution of C. Grant Loomis' *White Magic: An Introduction to the Folklore of Christian Legend* (Cambridge, MA: Medieval Academy of America, 1948). Of particular importance are Loomis' claims on magic as neither *maleficium* nor *beneficium* in and of itself. He asserts:

> Magic deals in wares not of a natural kind. Magic is a practice which seeks to turn events or control nature in an unnatural and unexpected fashion [...] Magic is knowledge beyond the average man's comprehension; it is a secret mastering influence which inspires wonder or fear [...] Magic is neither good nor evil in itself, for of itself it has no will...In religion, magic has at times assumed the aspect of a two-fold divinity [...]Magic is an operative force which has no prescribed intention, for magic in itself knows neither *maleficium* nor *beneficium*. (3)

Loomis is clear to posit the subject of magic, and white magic at that, in response to the wielder's or operator's heart, or seat of motive. Therefore, if the agent of magic is impoverished in heart and desires selfish acclaim, then the magic wielded will be constituted as black, or dark magic; however, if the agent of *beneficium* "pursues the ethics of kindness and goodness," it then reflects white magic, or the "acquisition of glory or power" (4).

1.4 A Quasi-Digression: a Pre-Modern Observation on Early Spanish Magic & Naturalis

John Locke (1632-1704), an epistemological political theorist commented on the subject matter of the miracle, and its relation to the supernatural event. The socio-historian Howard Clark Kee, in *Miracle in the Early Christian World* (herein, *Miracle*), relied rather heavily on Locke's explanation regarding miracles. Kee, has the following question from Locke:

> Though the common Experience and the Course of Things have justly a mighty Influence on the minds of men, to make them give or refuse Credit to anything proposed to their Belief; yet is there one Case wherein the strangeness of the Fact lessens not the Assent to a Fair Testimony given of it. For where such supernatural Events are suitable to ends aim'd at by him, who has the Power to change the course of Nature, there, under such circumstances, they may be fitter to procure Belief, by how much more they are beyond, or contrary to ordinary Observations. This is the proper Case of Miracles, which well attested, do not only find Credit themselves; but give it to other Truths which need such Confirmation. (6)[36]

The statement above is suggestive that He, who can change and alter Nature, is this subject's most important focus. Who or what could this be? Clearly, such a claim as the one above cannot stand on its own; i.e. it is in desperate need of context. Kee notes that Locke continues this trend of thought in a short work, *The Reasonableness of Christianity, as Delivered in the Scriptures* first published in 1695, wherein Locke posits the idea that "miracles are performed as evidence of Jesus' messiahship" (7). Perhaps though, miracles are not as distinct from magic after all. How so? Validation of the wielder of power is one thing, but that is not at stake, nor in question here. Jesus can still be a wonder worker, but he could also be construed to be a white magic operator of sorts; Jesus, man of wonders (*mirabilia*). Recall, this project thus far (or rather in this chapter) is concerned with expressing the complexity of the term "magic" and its affectations. We return to Locke as he provides a direct definition regarding the term "miracle," which is "a sensible operation, which, being above the comprehension of the spectator, and in his opinion contrary to the established course of nature, is taken him to be divine" (7). Of equal interest, and to further problematize the syntax of magic and miracle, Kee asserts, in his analysis of Locke, that "He [Locke] goes on to note that, since everyone judges which are nature's laws on the

---

[36] It should be noted that *The Works of John Locke*, 10 volumes (1823) is the source of Kee's analysis on Locke and miracles, specifically, "A Discourse on Miracles" (London, 1701).

basis of his own acquaintance with nature, what may be a miracle to one will
not be so to another" (7).

Contrastingly, David Hume (1711-1776), generally regarded as the most
important philosopher to write in the English language, offered another view
concerning the subject matter of miracles. Hume states, "a miracle is a
violation of natural law: and as a firm and unalterable experience has
established these laws, the proof against a miracle, from the very nature of
the fact, is as entire as any argument from experience can possibly be
imagined" (*Miracle* 11).[37] Hume relied more on the credibility of the teller
or performer of the miracle itself. Why? Because then "the testifier's
credibility was so great that it would be a greater miracle for him to tell a
falsehood" (11). I am not sure that such reasoning was altogether a logical
best option, but it does point to the thought of credibility, and Hume in this
regard was a skeptic of such a person in existence. At best, Hume was
anxious to link *mira*, or wonder alongside *miraculum*, or miracle stating, "If
the spirit of religion join itself to the love of wonder, there is an end of
common sense" (12). Such a claim was suggestive that those who
participated in such explanations of phenomena were marginalized, or were
to be marginalized and judged as other and barbaric.

What more can be stated as far as stories regarding the conjuring of
horses for travel, ships for sailing, invisibility and the invocation of
immortality, erotic and astral magic, experiments to afflict harm,
prescriptive necromantic manuals providing love potions and ageless
potions. Still, what of learned, demonic magic, adjurations, the use of herbs
and plants for health or for warding off disease, *dracontium* and mandrake
for sympathetic usage, examples of Marian devotion and the sign of the
cross which disturbed the distinction between traditional magic and
officially sanctioned blessings. Consequently, the disentanglement of magic
and religion and magic and science was not a very easy one, and was further
complicated as a shift toward expressions of the aforementioned were being
recorded in the literature of the culture, especially a Medieval Spain.

Jennifer M. Corry in her shaping work *Perceptions of Magic in Medieval
Spanish Literature* (herein, *Perceptions*) continues the aforementioned
thread that "magic…arose out of the human being's desire to gain more
control over Nature's immense forces and over Destiny" (202). Corry
further suggests a contested definition of magic against the Church, wherein
she posits the historical impact of both Church regulation and its attack on

---

[37] It is important to note that Kee is referencing the work of David Hume's *Enquiry
Concerning Human Understanding* (1748). The work is bifurcated in scope and
discusses: "Of Miracles" and "Of a Particular Providence and of a Future State,"
respectively.

other unofficial explanations of phenomena. Further, such an *ecclesia* ultimately "declared that there were only two forces in existence that could produce supernatural events: God and the Devil" (202). Again, belief sanctioned by the Church and official explanation took the form of *miraculum* versus *mira*. Corry states:

> When the Church began to evangelize throughout Pagan Europe, it considered magical practice a rival entity. At first, in order to compete, the Church incorporated many of the Pagan magical practices that it found into its own doctrine. It also began to create its own magic and called it *miracles*. As the Church grew in strength and gained the support of political leaders, it was able to declare heretical any practice it deemed unsuitable for its purposes. (202)

Conversely, Corry's accounting in her *Perceptions* recalls, from the earlier part of this initial chapter, the law of contraries. Here, she is consistent with the notion of "black" magic and its counterpart "white" magic via the creation of the Church. What is more, she continues this law of opposing binaries with the position of both the saint and the magician, albeit not a distinction any clearer than each respective wielder's ability to explain away phenomena, or influence their surroundings. Again, the "distinction," if any, lies within the context or realm of external power and/or influence. For Corry then:

> The Church had created the saints and holy people to serve as human agents through whom God could perform miracles…Christianity also created the saint's counterpart, the witch, through whom the Devil could perform his demonic magic. (203)

In a later chapter I share with Corry the idea that Spain held a higher tolerance than the remaining European continent during the thirteenth century, and this is due in part, to its intellectual history via the University, its literary output and treatment on the subject of magic, and a short-lived civil union amidst competing Jewish, Muslim, and Christian cultures.[38] Markedly, the literature of this period under the reign of Alfonso X and his court established a position of quasi-tolerance amidst the varied cultures in existence on the Iberian Peninsula; moreover, these cultures made up of Muslims, Jews and Christians found a common cause in the

---

[38] Of said competing cultures, further complications arise at the fruition of the Mozarabs, Iberian Peninsular Christians existing under Muslim surroundings and Conversos, Spanish converts from Judaism to Christianity; these too shall be briefly discussed in subsequent pages.

[un]organization of the translating centers that shifted focus from Seville toward Toledo and Castile.

CHAPTER TWO

Chapter 2 argues for why Spain may have held specific views on the subject of magic as a viable agent of study; specifically, discussing the repositories for the study of magic that gained a European continental focus at Salamanca, Córdoba, Valencia, Seville, and Toledo. Also, of considerable interest were the translating centers throughout these geographical regions and the important literature, which not only conveyed a quasi-tolerant culture amidst Muslims and Jews, but via such a medium, provided both a philosophical as well as a pragmatic examination of magic central toward an intellectual history of Spain.

Consequently, this second Chapter will briefly consider the vantage point and role of the University in Spain, and the categories of great, intellectual pursuit(s) one encountered in their [un]known world. Of these categories, the court of Alfonso X and his literature will be of most importance; i.e. these Alfonsan texts include selections of *Las Siete Partidas* and the *Lapidario*. Additionally, though we have previously examined the role of magic and science, it is imperative to look at the *Picatrix*, a text that received much attention by translators from the Arabic into the Latin. Moreover, what type of influence did each text convey to the Spanish culture at large? Were such texts [pre-]discussed in the setting of the academic University? Moreover, might their work betray an authorial classification as clergy, magician, or both, and what exactly were the advantages of such afore stated practitioners during the thirteenth century? These inquiries begin the examination of magic as a viable subject, and not the mere object of curiosity; at once, the role of magic and its perception stand as referents to comprehending the [un]seen world, realm, and perhaps even one's condition for being.[1]

---

[1] I am here not solely referring to an existential position as suggested by Kierkegaard and followed via Heidegger, Sartre, and Camus; we are moving beyond the metaphysical, but still paying homage to its inception.

2.1 A Birth of the University & "Caves" of Learning in Spain

The position of the University was two-fold in thirteenth century Spain. First, it was a physical gathering space where learning and translating from Arabic and Hebrew texts into the Latin was common and necessary. Second, the position of intellectual rigor, though usually held by the clergy and those with a like-minded, literate disposition, began with an idealized dream for the unification of the Spanish people. As we shall later note, the conflation of foreign ideas amidst local color allowed Alfonso X to contribute to an Iberian intellectual history that remains an important factor until this very day.[2] Though the formation of learning is usually attributed to both Paris and Oxford as early institutions of higher learning, the *Columbia Encyclopedia*, sixth edition (New York: Columbia UP, 2005)[3] has noted that:

> The Moors were driven out in 1085. Salamanca became world famous after the foundation (1218) of its university by Alfonso IX. The university soon rivaled Bologna, Paris, and Oxford, and it made Arabic philosophy available to the Western world. In the late Middle Ages and throughout the Renaissance, Salamanca was the center of Christian Spanish cultural life and the fountainhead of Spanish theology.

Salamanca, a land rich in history and lore located west of central Spain, in Castile-León, on the Tormes River was recalled by the poet Unamuno as:

> Y este cielo, tu prez y tu dicha,
> *Salamanca,*
> es el cielo que esmalta tus piedras
> con oro de siglos.
> Como el poso del cielo en la tierra

---

[2] The *Siete Partidas* of Alfonso X never obtained the national application that the king envisioned within his lifetime, and in fact did not receive such respect until the fourteenth century under Alfonso XI (c.a. 1311-1350). Further, the *Partidas'* influence on the U.S. frontier was legion; According to Robert I. Burns, S.J. "The *Partidas* did not work its *magic* in the New World as the direct and primary law of the land but rather as a living component of the developing Spanish codes, surviving as a main root, as foundation and principles, and as supplementary law" (*Las Siete Partidas*, trans., Samuel Parsons Scott, ed. Robert I. Burns, S.J., 5 vols. (Philadelphia: University of Pennsylvania Press, 2001), 1:xix.. Still, the *Partidas* held considerable effect and influence in the Law of Louisiana, Texas, California, and in the Southwest Mining and Water Law (1:xix-xxix).
[3] "Salamanca, city, Spain." *The Columbia Encyclopedia,* 6th ed. New York: Columbia University Press, 2001–04. www.bartleby.com/65/. 15 June 2007.

resplende tu pompa,
Salamanca.

And this sky, your worth and your happiness,
Salamanca,
is the sky that enamels your stones
with centuries of gold.
As the depths of heavens in the earth
reflect your pomp [perhaps, *glory*],
Salamanca.

Further, it was Alfonso IX who made it possible for the University of Salamanca to exist as a rather "safe zone," wherein all were welcomed and disputes amongst students and Masters could be resolved via the clergy and local magistrates. According to Manuel Gonzalez Garcia's, "Salamanca en la Baja Edad Media" (herein, "Salamanca") in Álvarez's edited series *Los Traductores*, he asserts:

El, [Alfonso IX] a su vez, ofrece protección a cuantos quieran venir a Salamanca a estudiar. Los estudiantes han de tener paz entre ellos y con los vecinos de la villa. Si surge alguna disputa, ésta sería vista por un tribunal constituido por clérigos y seglares. (126)

He, [Alfonso IX] at the same time, offers protection to as many who desire to come to Salamanca to study. The students should have peace among them and with the neighbors of the village. If some dispute arises, this will be overseen by a court or tribunal constituted of both clergymen and secular authorities.[4]

The zeal of such a Spanish king continued into the reign of Alfonso X, *El Sabio*, or the Wise One. Again, we turn to Garcia's commentary. He states, "De todos los reyes castellanos, el que más estrechamente ha quedado unido a la Universidad de Salamanca ha sido Alfonso X, por su decidida protección al Estudio salmantino," ["Of all the Castilian kings, the one who has remained most closely linked to the University of Salamanca has been Alfonso X, because of his decisive protection of salamancan study"] (126). The school at Salamanca then recognized both a Catholic appeal as well as a secular plea to uniformity. As Garcia notes, such a time was indeed "uno de influjo real y otro eclesiástico," ["one of royal influx and the other of Church

---

[4] Unless otherwise mentioned, the Spanish to English translations are my own.

influence"] (128).[5] It is because of such a conflation of influences, however
that one went to school in the first place to learn the seven liberal arts, and to

---

[5] Garcia further suggests that this concurrence of royal and ecclesiastical influence
upon the school at Salamanca although there from the beginning, was not the main
reason for its inception. In fact, as Garcia states:

>   El origen de la Universidad salmantina guarda alguna relación con la escuela
>   catedralicia, cuya existencia ya consta desde mediados del siglo XII. Pero la
>   Universidad de Salamanca fue creada por una decisión real y no por una
>   disposición pontifica o eclesiástica.
>
>   No se sabe cual fue la actitud de Alfonso IX en relación con la escuela
>   catedralicia: si la separó de la catedral y creó con ella la Universidad, o si el
>   rey, por su parte, creó un centro distinto y luego le añadió la escuela
>   catedralicia. (128)

>   The origin of the Salamancan University kept some relation with the
>   cathedral school, whose existence is known from the middle of the XII
>   century. But the University of Salamanca was created by a real decision and
>   not by pontifical or church regulation.
>
>   We do not know what the attitude of Alfonso IX was exactly, with
>   regards to the cathedral school: if he separated it from the cathedral tradition
>   and created with her the University, or if the king, for his part, created a
>   distinct center and later added the cathedral school.

It is not until we read further into Garcia's analysis that we find the historian
suggesting the following, and I quote it here at length:

>   Probablemente, el origen real de la Universidad, así como el impacto que
>   estaba produciendo el derecho romano, marcaron la orientación de los
>   estudios en esta primera etapa medieval de la Universidad. "La fama de
>   Salamanca medieval fue también casi enteramente la de una escuela de leyes
>   civiles y canónicas".(128).

>   Probably, the royal origin of the University, in the same way the impact
>   that was producing the Roman Law, established the direction of studies in
>   this first medieval stage of the University. "The fame of Medieval Salamanca
>   was also, almost entirely so, a school whose central focus concerned both
>   canonical and civil laws."

From such an analysis it is possible to track the battle lines between Church and local
order and influence. Still, the emergence of "la nueva etapa de la Universidad tiene
su expression externa en la formalizacion de la facultad de Teologia," ["the new
phase of the University has its external expression in the formalization of the faculty
of Theology"] (*Salamanca* 129). This was to become the impetus for higher
education, because rigorous training was for the advancement of the Church. And,
again those who participated were of the literate class and caste. Of further interest
was the role of the University for its markedly homage response to its faculties of
Canon Law and Civil Law, albeit the Roman right, or law. As we shall note,
Alphonso X's *Las Siete Partidas* (*Partidas*) is based on Roman Civil Law.

appreciate other subject materials of learning such as, say magic. A final note regarding education and its inception of systematic learning and space considers the role of jurisdiction and economics. Once more we turn to Manuel Gonzalez Garcia. He claims:

> Este periodo se caracteriza por una mayor dependencia de la jurisdicción de la Iglesia. Paralelamente, aumento por una mayor dependencia económica de los estudiantes respecto de la Iglesia, ya que los reyes se inhiben ante la enseñanza por el elevado gasto que supone. Finalmente, con este referendo del papa, la Universidad de Salamanca paso a formar parte de la comunidad intelectual de las universidades de occidente (Paris, Bolonia, Oxford), que tenia su origen en la intervención e influjo de la Santa Sede. (*Salamanca* 129)

> This period [late twelfth to early thirteenth century] is characterized by a greater dependence regarding the jurisdiction of the Church. In a parallel fashion, there increases a greater economic dependence of the students with respect to the Church, since the kings did not involve themselves in the teaching because of the elevated expense that it supposed. Finally, with this referendum from the Pope, the University of Salamanca proceeded to form part of the intellectual community of the universities of the West (Paris, Bologna, Oxford), that had its origin in the intervention and influence of the Holy See.

Did such Church influence extend into other areas of Spain and was its influence upon an intellectual culture advantageous? From Manuel Gonzalez Garcia we turn our gaze south to the region of Andalusia, specifically the land known as Córdoba.

Córdoba, located in the south of Spain, in Andalusia, on the Guadalquivir River, "flourished under the Romans, then passed to the Visigoths (572) and the Moors (711), and again under the Umayyad dynasty became the seat (756–1031) of an independent emirate, later called caliphate, which included most of Muslim Spain" ("Cordoba," www.bartleby.com/65/). The city itself became a center for cooperation amidst variant religious and secular orders; a position that allowed "the city" to become "then one of the greatest and wealthiest in Europe, renowned as a center of Muslim and Jewish culture" ("Cordoba," www.bartleby.com/65/). At the crossroads of Muslim and Jewish custom a subject such as "magic" could not only flourish alongside other arts of learning, but due to such a high affinity for the conflation of cultural ideals (philosophy, cultural artifacts, et cetera), and additionally—due to overlapping and augmentation

per people group(s), a level of syncretism was, arguably, foreseeable .[6] What
is more, the southern region boasted trade with the North African routes of
goods that crossed the Mediterranean, and as such Córdoba (in some cases
seen as Córdova) benefited immensely from the abundance of such
prevalent gold shipments. As historian Angus McKay comments in *Spain in
the Middle Ages: from Frontier to Empire, 1000-1500* (herein, *Spain in the
Middle Ages*), "Córdoba was…outstanding for its cosmopolitan and cultural
atmosphere: it was an intellectual center as well as being the capital of the
caliphate" (8). What is of interest here is the problem that the caliphate
presented regarding those committed to unification; a position that
continuously caused unrest and leadership schism within the royal class,
(namely the political inefficacy of Alfonso X) for a land, in which McKay
further suggests, "environmental features encouraged regional autonomy"
(8). Moreover, communication in the midst of mountainous terrain and
unnavigable rivers as well as racial and tribal conflict also plagued not only
Córdoba, but most of central to southern Spain (McKay). Hence, such
geographical diversity made matters difficult for those seeking a unified
Spain. In many cases, Córdoba, according to D. Pedro de Madrazo, in his,
"El Siglo XIII: fe y tolerancia: asociación de elementos opuestos.—
Sincronismos.—Fundación de la Capilla Real," (herein, "El Siglo"),[7]
comments on Christian faith and tolerance in the midst of competing
cultures of both the Muslim and the Jewish tradition; this contention of
cultures allowed for the presentation not only of each groups' respective
point of view, but also allowed for some to choose the best of all three,
thereby creating a syncretic, cultural ideal. Madrazo reminds us and even
places himself in the conversation, referring to himself in the third person,
he states, "La aficion a las ideas y costumbres islamitas no es, como
vulgarmente se cree, carácter distintivo y peculiar […] No es solo D. Pedro
el que prefiere la cultura morisca a la cristiana," ["the liking for Islamic
ideas and customs is not, as is erroneously believed, of a distinct and
peculiar nature […] It is not only D. Pedro who prefers the Moorish culture
to the Christian one"] ("El Siglo" 303). Because of such a rich entangling of
cultures and belief systems, arguably, all of Spain, became a breeding
ground for *la era moderna*, or the modern era, which "entre nosotros"
(between "us," or in this case—first the Cordobans, then the remainder of

---

[6] It should be noted that "magic" as I reference it here may be construed as a matter
of perspective; i.e. the texts of Muslim and Hebrew mystical works were often
regarded as "magic" and "superstition" by Christian observers, especially the esoteric
texts of the Kabala tradtion.
[7] This chapter essay is taken from *Córdoba. España: Sus Monumentos y Artes-su
Naturaleza é Historia: Córdoba* (Barcelona: D. Cortezo y ca., 1884).

Spain) became "la expresion de todas las grandes ideas socials: la religión, la política, la literatura, el arte," ["the expression of all the big, social ideas: religion, politics, literature, the arts"] (303). Where do we note such parameters at work in a common goal exactly? It is to be found in the establishing of opposition and unification within that antagonism of expressed social ideals regarding religion and politics and literature and of course the post-Aristotelian notion of the arts. Again, we turn to Madrazo's recounting of such ideation, and I quote it here at length:

> En el siglo que inaugura la era moderna […] la religión, la política, la literatura, el arte, se formulan de dos maneras enteramente opuestas en la corte y entre el pueblo; formula nacional y popular, católica, exclusista y celosa, por un lado; formula de corte y gabinete, filosófica, reformista, incrédula, tolerante y sin celo, por el otro. ("El Siglo" 303)

> In the century [late XIII-early XIV] that inaugurates the modern era […] religion, politics, literature, art, formulate in two ways that are completely contrary in the court and among the people; national and popular, the position catholic, exclusionary and jealous, on the one hand; the position of the court and cabinet, philosophical, reformist, sceptical, tolerant and without zeal, on the other.

Madrazo seemingly continues his point by point categorizing and settles on this project's relevant topic, namely the position of literature in such a heterogeneous society. With reference to both the court and the nation—he asserts:

> La corte ama una literatura impregnada de sensualismo y un arte seductor y pagano, y la nación prefiere la nervuda y varonil literatura de sus romances y el arte austero, místico y sombrío, florecido a la sombra de los claustros. (303)

> The court loves a literature impregnated with sensuality and a seductive and pagan art, while the nation prefers a sinewy and manly literature with respect to its romances and their austere art, mystical and somber [in tone], thriving in the shade of the cloisters [of the Church].

Though such cultural distinctions, according to Madrazo's account, provide a prescription for an either— or scenario with regards to Muslims and Christians living in close proximity, we turn again to a more, recent critic. Historian Angus McKay argues that towards the third quarter of the thirteenth century, the subject of tolerance for religious alterity resonated "according to the degree of resistance offered to the Christians and the strategic value of key areas" (*Spain in the Middle Ages* 68). Still, the position of *tolerance* was a viable stasis of cultural behavior and appeal amongst mozarabs,[8] Christians and Jews, namely as we shall note the Jews of Toledo and their use of Arabic for their "private" writing.[9] Of further interest, regarding both the role of knowledge and the phenomena of translation from Arabic into Latin and Spanish, McKay reminds us of such intellectual contributions as the translation of the fundamental work of Greek astronomy, Ptolemy's *Almagest* (c.a 150). This Latin translation of the *Almagest* was drawn upon extensively by Alfonso X and the scholarship and translation was out of his court. However, as McKay continues, "the scholars of Islam [stemming from Baghdad and Córdoba] were not merely translators," but in fact became, even in Seville, poets themselves amidst "Greek science and philosophy within an Islamic and Arabic-language setting" (82-83).[10] We now shift our attention slightly from Córdoba and travel back North just shy of Salamanca where we find Toledo and its school of *traductores*, or translators.

Toledo, located in central Spain, in Castile–La Mancha, is on a granite hill surrounded on three sides by a gorge of the Tagus River; historically and culturally, it is one of the most important cities within all of Spain. Under Moorish rule (c.a. 712–1085), Toledo flourished and welcomed Spanish, Muslim and Jewish people who lived within close proximity of each other, and hence the city became a great translating center and a place of somewhat

---

[8] Simply put the *mozarabs* were Iberian Christians who lived under Muslim rule in al-Andalus; their progeny further retained the Christian tradition and influence, and as such became a localized, autonomous community of their own. One can imagine living in the eleventh through thirteenth century and contributing to an Iberian socio-political tradition replete with Muslim, Jewish and especially Christian *traditio*. The effect would cause for an amalgamation of culture and an aggregation of whatever it meant to be *Spanish*. It should be noted that the *mozarabs*, although Christian, were presumably attracted to many aspects of the Arab and Islamic civilization. And as is commonly known the [mozarabs] were by no means hostile to Muslim rule, but learnt Arabic (though they also spoke a Romance dialect) and adopted many Arab customs.

[9] For further reading concerning the Mozarabic atmosphere and the secrets of Arab science and the prelates regarding the new science, which had the support of the bishops of Toledo via "schools" of learning see José M. Millás Vallicrosa, *Las Traducciones orientales en los manuscriptos de la Biblioteca Catedral de Toledo* (Madrid: Instituto Arias Montano, 1942).

[10] McKay notes that while Greek scientific texts were studied without question in the Islamic world, the study of Greek philosophy was somewhat more problematic: "In contrast to subjects such as mathematics, astronomy, and medicine, the study of Greek philosophy appeared dangerous to *Qur'-ān*-centered theology because it claimed to demonstrate truths in much the same way as the Greek empirical sciences did" (*Spain in the Middle Ages*), [New York: MacMillan P, 1977], 84.

tolerant, intellectual activity. According to Ana María López Álvarez from the Museo Safardi, under Muslim rule, Toledo's fame was at its highest point during the tenth century, but the city reached its apogee during the reign of Alfonso X *el Sabio*, during the thirteenth century; the former stemming from the "grandeza de al-Andalus durante la época del califato," ["greatness of al-Andalus during the epoch of the caliphate"] while the latter resulted from "varios focos en la España cristiana," ["various focuses in Christian Spain"] (*La Escuela de Traductores de Toledo* 9). The end result proved to be a shift "por Toledo en el desarollo de al-Andalus...una vez caído el califato los hombres de ciencia y poetas se agruparon al lado de los reyes taifas," ["for Toledo in the disarray of al-Andalus...once the fall of the caliphate took place these men of science and poets gathered together on the side of the *ta'ifah* kings"] (9).[11] The Arabic influence was heavy in Toledo and infused itself upon its cultural landscape affecting its inhabitants along the way. Álvarez asserts, "lo árabe ejerce en las costumbres, modas, modos de vida, así como en los contenidos y temática de la literatura de los judíos españoles y que se refleja en la poesía, gramática, exégesis y en la filosofía," ["Arabic influence exerts itself on the customs, fashions, lifestyles, as well as in the contents and the subject matter of Spanish Jewish Literature and it is reflected in poetry, grammar, exegesis and in philosophy"] (9). Texts that were likely to be translated were primarily those scientific texts concerning the explanation of phenomena and healing (medicine) as well as Arabic philosophy that were brought to al-Andalus.[12] Where the presentation of

---

[11] In translating the term, *taifas*, we should note that the term in Arabic is *ta'ifah*, and holds no parallel one word English translation; however, perhaps the following selection taken from the 2007 edition of the *Encyclopedia Britannica* can best elucidate the term as follows:

A faction or party, as applied to the followers of any of the petty kings who appeared in Muslim Spain in a period of great political fragmentation early in the 11th century after the dissolution of the central authority of the Umayyad caliphate of Córdoba. After the dictatorship of al-Muzaffar (reigned 1002–08), civil war reduced the caliphate to a puppet institution.

This article is taken from "taifa," *Encyclopædia Britannica*. 2007. *Encyclopædia Britannica* Online. 15 June 2007 <http://www.britannica.com/eb/article-9070959>. Thereby, creating a further layer to the already anxious and apprehensive levels, regarding local and "soverign" authority, for the unification of the Iberian people; further, I resist the temptation to call them, or these people—"Spaniards," for Spain at this period [eleventh through the late thirteenth century] was still oscillating in its identity.

[12] Julio Samso in his chapter from *La Escuela de Traductores de Toledo*, "Las traducciones toledanas en los siglos XII-XIII" asserts, "durante el periodo taifa, esta ciudad [Toledo] conoció un desarrollo científico extraordinario en el campo de la

multi-lingual literature and culture allowed for overlapping participation, some critics have suggested at least for this time period on the Iberian Peninsula, specifically in Toledo from the tenth century to the thirteenth century, that not only did a fair tolerance amidst such varied and competing groups exist, but also within this context, an appreciation for difference, though short-lived, could be tracked and measured in the literary works themselves. That is, Jews were translating Arabic works and Spanish *conversos*, or Spanish Jews who became Christians were translating Hebrew and Latin texts into Spanish. And, according to Ángel Sáenz-Badillos in his, "Participación de judíos en las traducciones de Toledo"[13]: "En ninguna otra ciudad europea o peninsular se daba una mezcla cultural tan variada y tan llena de vida como en Toledo," ["In no other European or peninsular city was there such a cultural mixture so varied and so full of life as in Toledo"]. What exactly did such advantages mean linguistically? Again, we turn to Sáenz-Badillas who states, "El ambiente lingüístico de la ciudad ofrecía una variedad curiosa y atrayente, en la que el bilingüismo y aun el trilingüismo estaban a la orden del día," ["The linguistic environment of the city presented a curious and appealing variety, in that bilingualism and even trilingualism were the order of the day"] (65). Toledo at its height, like Córdoba and Salamanca, represented the integrated and cultural best of the Iberian Peninsula where subjects as disparate in form and practice flourished, and translators, in keeping with Graeco-Arab tradition, found intellectual pasture, albeit a fruitful locus by which historian Samuel M. Waxman, in his *Chapters on Magic in Spanish Literature* (herein, *Chapters*), (1916), admittedly posits that, "The study of magic during the Middle Ages was regarded as a legitimate intellectual pursuit. It [magic] was

---

astronomía y en el de la agronomía," ["during the period of *ta'ifah* rule, this city [Toledo] saw an extraordinary scientific development in the field of Astronomy and of Agronomy"] (17). During such a period of intellectual development it is clear that the distinctions between what were magic or magical and what was supposedly integrated as scientific discovery were not readily discernable. What is more, in one example, Samso extends in a prescriptive manner the thematic interests that translators from the Toledo school were involved with, specifically when translating the *Almagest*; Gerard of Cremona (c. 1114-1187) was one of the most famous scholars who came to Toledo, and besides his translation of Ptolemy, Gerard translated more than eighty-one works which covered fields such as: "la Lógica, Filosofía, Matemática, Óptica, Dinámica, Astronomía y Astrología, Medicina, Alquimia, Geomancia y otros sistemas de adivinación," ["Logic, Philosophy, Mathematics, Optics, Dynamics, Astronomy and Astrology, Medicine, Alchemy, Geomancy and other systems of Divination"] (20).
[13] In *La Escuela de Traductores de Toledo*, ed. Ana María López Álvarez (Toledo: Diputación Provincial de Toledo, 1996), 65-70.

even sometimes classed as one of the seven liberal arts," and again that "the most renowned of all [schools for the study of magic] were in Spain at Toledo, Seville, Cordova, and Salamanca" (1-2). Waxman, in his *Chapters*, quickly shifts to his examination of Spanish literature by suggesting that Arabs and Jews were responsible for keeping such a subject aflame and, that "The Arabs had brought along with them from the East their traditions which had a strong magical flavor" (3). Such a magical aura manifested itself in the sciences as mathematics, astrology, astronomy, and alchemy and "were closely associated with magic both black and white" (2).[14]

Further, such subjects of study came under heavy, ecclesiastical attack, and in addition to learning spaces such as translating centers, the invention of the cave[s] of learning became an extended, mythical locus of learning as well—preserved in literary accounts.[15] Stories of *cult* wisdom and the praxis of magic and the dark arts, lore and legend closely followed. As Samuel M. Waxman asserts:

> Magic in all ages having been frowned upon by the ecclesiastical authorities, its study was assumed to have been conducted clandestinely. Therefore a cave was invented, not at all an unlikely place for the pursuit of forbidden study [...] since the study of black magic presupposed dealings with the devil who dwelt in the infernal regions, an underground school would seem entirely appropriate. (6-7)

---

[14] Samuel M. Waxman suggests that there was a faint and practical distinction regarding the "white" and "black" magic ideal, and the affectations that went along with this respective bifurcation and its subsequent performance. He asserts, "This subtle distinction between the study and the practice of magic seems to have been universal in the Middle Ages and it was probably responsible for the two classifications, white and black magic" (*Chapters* 1).

[15] According to Antonio Garrosa Resina it was in Toledo that stories involving "la Cueva de Hércules," ["the Cave of Hercules"] surged and circulated. He further suggests that alongside this legend of the cave, the most famous cave of learning existed in Salamanca, and was simply noted as "la famosa Cueva de Salamanca," which inspired several literary works stemming from the *Siglo de Oro* (*Magia y Superstición Magia y Supersticion en la Literatura Castellana Medieval* (Valladolid: Universidad de Valladolid, Secretariado de Publicaciones, 1987, 38-39).

And due to the geography of Toledo, the legend of a cave[16] found credible, fertile soil in the minds of the curious. Though Waxman presents solid scholarship concerning the subject of magic in Spain, we now turn to more recent study of the subject of magic as presented by Spanish literary critic and historian, Antonio Garrosa Resina in his *Magia y Superstición en la literatura Castellana Medieval* (1987) (hereafter, *Magia y Superstición*). Garrosa Resina provides a worthy introduction to the position of Spanish Literature and its expression concerning the subject of magic, religion and culture. Garrosa Resina suggests:

> Todos los pueblos han tenido, en sus creencias, un primer principio, un Dios; en todas las sociedades, algunos individuos se han apartado de la creencia general y han acuñado formas especiales [...] Cuando ese pueblo ha sido conquistado por otro, o cuando un nuevo sistema religioso se ha impuesto por diversas razones—políticas, morales, de aculturación—, han quedado subyacentes ritos, fiestas, usos, costumbres que en forma de substrato permanecen deformado la vida religiosa del pueblo a través de la historia. (15)

> All people have had, in their beliefs, a primary principle, a God; in all societies, some individuals have departed from the general belief and have coined special forms [...] When such a people have been conquered by another, or when some new religious system has imposed itself for diverse reasons—political, ethical, the result of acculturation—, what remained has been the underlying rituals, festivals, uses, customs, which in their substratum form remain deformed, via the religious life of the people throughout their history.[17]

---

[16] The advantages of receiving knowledge were, according to Waxman, that one "would become omniscient" an attribute that belonged to the Divine Nature. This further problematized the position of the study of magic as being something opposed to the institution and the theology of accepted Church doctrine. Moreover, the one who gathered such dark knowledge just "might learn the speech of birds, the power to dominate wind and sea and all the forces of nature" (*Chapters* 17). Where Nature then played a subservient role outside the Divine influence, the "professor of magic was the devil himself" (22). Clearly, such tutees became proficient in the arts and claimed knowledge beyond the natural realm. Why? Waxman asserts, "It was common belief in the Middle Ages that all magicians derived their knowledge of the black arts from the Prince of Darkness, and the closer their relations with the devil the greater their proficiency," and moreover, such a price for admission into this black exchange, "was popularly supposed to have been the soul of the student" (23).
[17] *Magia y Supersticion en la Literatura Castellana Medieval* (Valladolid: Universidad de Valladolid, Secretariado de Publicaciones, 1987), 7.

What Garrosa Resina suggests is that such a conquered people would retain, as a residue, their former culture, and that such a mixture might produce a space for frequent manifestations of the supernatural. Arguably, such a "space" may find rich soil in which to prosper through the official religion and the written literature. Further, Garrosa Resina asserts:

> Esto es lo que da lugar a las supersticiones con harta frecuencia. Su reflejo se muestra en la vida corriente y con gran amplitud en el saber popular que—al desfolklorizarse—pasa a la literatura escrita. (7)

> This is what gives place to superstitions with extreme frequency. Its reflection is displayed in the common, normal life and with great amplitude in the popular knowledge that—as it undergoes a process of losing its popular currency—passes on to the written literature.

Here, Garrosa Resina is referring to the forms of superstition that find a metamorphosed foothold in the middle of a belief system; in this case, he asserts, "Estas supersticiones perviven, frecuentemente, metamorfoseadas por la religion official," ["These superstitions survive, rather frequently, metamorphosed by the official religion"] (7). Garrosa Resina, in observing the topic of magic in Spanish Literature in the Castilian language, suggests that the scholarship on the subject matter of its expression, is at once impoverished and quasi-virginal. In his introduction to the position of magic his approach, though initially chastising, remains hopeful exemplary as he states:

> De toda la producción literaria en lengua castellana, la correspondiente a la época medieval es seguramente la que menos ha atraído la atención de los estudiosos. Y a esta parcela bastante descuidada de nuestras letras dedicamos ahora este trabajo, que se centrará en el estudio de un aspecto tan sugerente cuanto desconocido: las manifestaciones de la magia y la superstición que afloran en los textos literarios medievales. (11)

> Of all the literary production in the Castilian [Spanish] language, that corresponding to the medieval period is surely the one that has attracted the least attention of scholars. And to this quite neglected field of our letters we dedicate now this work, that will be centered in the study of an aspect as much suggestive as unknown: the expressions of magic and superstition that surface in medieval literary texts.

Seen here, the aforementioned is more than a mere disclaimer and regards the scope for his book via reference of such *siglos*, or centuries from the thirteenth to the fifteenth century. However, we are concerned with his criticism involving the generalization of magic, as well as the position of magic in the thirteenth century as expressed in Spanish Literature. In utilizing Samuel M. Waxman's criticism on the subject, even Garrosa Resina acknowledges his contribution to the topic at hand with reference to the legend of the magician, wielder and demonstrator of the magical arts. He states, "Por su parte Waxman, en su estudio *Chapters on Magic in Spanish Literature*, hablando en esta misma línea de la leyenda de Gerberto, recoge la opinión de que este, going to Seville he practiced there divinations and indications as was the custom among the Saracens," ["For his part Waxman, in his study *Chapters on Magic in Spanish Literature*, speaking along this line of the legend of Gerberto, includes the opinion that with this, 'going to Seville he practiced there divinations and indications as was the custom among the Saracens'"] (35). In acknowledging Waxman's contribution to the subject of magic as a learned craft, and the practitioner of such an "art," as wielder of immense influence—Garrosa Resina further cements his observation of magic and the magician via an examination of Spanish cities and their magical traditions. He states, "Todas las naciones europeas tuvieron durante la Edad Media algunas ciudades donde se cultiva la magia de forma especial," ["All of the European Nations had during the Middle Ages some cities where magic was cultivated in special ways"] (37). Moreover, special locations, or spaces are included such as the University, as we have already noted. Garrosa Resina explains:

> Sabemos que en Francia esta suerte le cupo a la ciudad de Orleáns, mientras que en Italia la compartieron Padua, con su famosa Universidad, y Nápoles, mas en contacto con la civilización musulmana y los núcleos árabes de Sicilia. Pero en ningún país esta localización geográfica tuvo tanta importancia como en España, donde Toledo, Córdoba, Sevilla, y mas tarde Salamanca, adquirieron una fama que pronto se extendió por toda Europa, de forma que el continente vio en España el centro de los estudios de las artes negras a lo largo de la Edad Media. (37)

> We know that in France this classification belongs to the city of Orleáns, while in Italy it is shared between Padua, with its famous University, and Naples, more in contact with the Moslem civilization and the Arabian groups of Sicily. But in no other country did this geographical localization have as much importance as in Spain, where Toledo, Córdoba, Seville, and later Salamanca, acquired a fame that soon itself extended throughout all of Europe, so much so that the continent saw in Spain the center for the studies of the black arts throughout a good portion of the Middle Ages.

Though Garrosa Resina asserts that Toledo held the most prestige when it came to its ubiquity as a center for the study of "magic," he is well aware of the importance of Córdoba, Seville and other cities as centers for the study of magic. These areas of learning created a rich environment for the incorporation of magic within the "curricula" that included the *trivium* as well as the *quadrivium*. Garrosa Resina asserts:

> Durante los siglos peores de postración cultural del occidente cristiano, árabes y judíos mantuvieron inapagada en España la llama de la enseñanza, y puesto que la magia se asocio íntimamente con el estudio de las ciencias como matemáticas, astronomía, astrología, medicina y alquimia, en las sobresalieron los sabios árabes, es natural que España cobrara dicha reputación.

> Toledo, Córdoba y Sevilla fueron los grandes focos culturales de la España musulmana y por ello adquirieron, mas que otras ciudades, intensa fama de centros de magia. Cuando a fines del siglo XIII, Salamanca, tras la fundación de su famosa Universidad, se convirtió en el centro cultural por excelencia de la España cristiana, se la asocio también con el estudio de la magia. (37)

> During the worst centuries of cultural prostration of the Christian West, Arabs and Jews maintained un-extinguished in Spain the flame of teaching, and the position of magic itself became intimately associated with the study of the sciences such as mathematics, astronomy, astrology, medicine and alchemy, in which the wise Arabs excelled, it is indeed only natural that Spain acquired for itself the aforesaid reputation.

> Toledo, Córdoba and Seville were the large cultural foci of Moslem Spain and because of it they acquired, more than any other cities, intense fame for their schools of magic. When at the end of the XIII century, Salamanca, after the foundation of its famous University, became the cultural center par excellence of Christian Spain, it too became associated with the study of the magic.

Interestingly, as we have previously examined, the position of magic in Spain during the thirteenth century was embedded within the seven liberal arts and reflected the cultural milieu during this time period. However, in studying magic Garrosa Resina asserts that it is the dark arts that receive attention; what about the study and practice of the arts, which produced a positive effect, or what C. Loomis termed, *beneficium*, or "white" magic. We turn once more to Garrosa Resina as he suggests that there is a distinction between "white" magic and "black" magic. Concerning magic in general Garrosa Resina states:

> Magia, en general…es una ilusión que consiste en pretender dominar la naturaleza (y en ocasiones también a las fuerzas sobrenaturales) mediante determinados actos en los que se usa de un supuesto poder coercitivo propio del hombre y que se supone existe en mayor o menor cantidad, según los individuos. (15)

Magic, in general…is an illusion which consists in pretending to dominate Nature (and on occasion also supernatural forces) by means of determinant acts via the use of supposed, coercive powers of an individual and that supposedly exist in major and minor quantities, depending on the person.

Such coercive tactics then materialize in the forms of a "good" and a "bad" usage of influence, wherein Garrosa Resina further comments on the motive involved with each bifurcated element of magic. He suggests:

Atendiendo al fin perseguido por la práctica mágica, según que este sea bueno o malo, hablaremos de magia blanca o benéfica y de magia negra o maléfica. Pero esta división no resulta en ocasiones muy precisa, porque un mismo individuo puede, según se lo aconsejen las circunstancias o sus deseos, practicar la magia negra para inferir cualquier clase de mal a otra persona. Si consideramos que lo más importante de la magia es el resultado práctico que esta se propone, la clasificación más rentable será la que atiende a la naturaleza y orientación de los fines. (16)

Given the end pursued by the practice of magic, according to which it may be "good" or a "bad," we will speak of white or beneficial magic [*beneficium*] and of black or harmful magic [*maleficium*]. But this division does not result from very specific situations, because the same individual is able, according to what the circumstances may suggest or his desires, to practice black magic to inflict any kind of evil on another person. If we consider that the most important thing about magic is the practical result that it proposes, the most worthwhile classification will be the one that keeps in mind to the nature and orientation of the end.

What Garrosa Resina brings up is of interest for a future project, namely the practicality of magic, or put in a more positive sense, the pragmatism of the uses and performance of magic in its bifurcated forms. We are not concerned with this directly, however, in part because it is not the scope for this project, though it does merit further investigation.

The study of Astronomy manifested itself in the seven liberal arts, and the infusion of magic and divination found equal participation in its craft. Intrigued, students came to the varied translating centers that afforded both a space for scholarship and the understanding or comprehension of one's world via the stars, planets and other heavenly bodies. Garrosa Resina agrees that the study of Astrology readily found an audience, but also: "De otro lado, la magia tenia sus adeptos y practicantes en todas las clases socials," ["On the other hand, magic had its followers and practitioners in all of the social classes"] (31). Hence, where both king and scholars and the courts participated, magic and its study prospered; such an output flourished in the annals of the scientific and the historical texts and codes alike; the former concerns the *Picatrix*, a manuscript on Astrology and the science of magic; the latter, gives reference to Alfonso X, his court and his works, namely the magnanimous *Siete Partidas* and the shorter *Lapidario*.

2.2 The Position of Translation & Translation Centers in Spain

Spain became a translating center during the Middle Ages, specifically from the eleventh through the thirteenth century. Arab settlers brought their trade and culture to the Iberian Peninsula. In turn, translators, looking to comprehend and apply much of Arabic scholarship, translated original works in Arabic and Greek texts existing in Arabic translation into Latin and Spanish. One of the more important of such texts is the *Picatrix*.

The *Picatrix* was translated from Arabic for Alfonso *el Sabio* in c.a. 1256. It is an introduction to magic, which treats the subject as if it were a science. The actual author of the *Picatrix* is unknown, although the treatise has been falsely attached to the Andalusian mathematician and astronomer Abū al-Qāsim Maslama ibn Aḥmad al Faraḍī (†1070) from Madrid and usually referred to as al-Maǧrīṭī ("the one from Madrid"), although he spent his productive life in Córdoba where he established a school of learning. The suggestion that the name *Picatrix* is derived from the Arabic word for Hippocrates ("Biqraṭīs") has now been abandoned in favor of an hypothesis that derives *Picatrix* from a Spanish feminine noun "picatriz" ("one who bites"), itself a calgue of the root *m-s-l* ("to bite"), interpreted as the base of al-Maǧrīṭī's "surname," Maslama (interpreted as grammatically feminine because of its –a ending).[18]

The *Picatrix* translated as a matter of national and cultural importance via the auspices of the Alfonsan court in the thirteenth century. Alfonso X, in catering to his native language, ordered that the Arabic text be translated not in the *lingua* Latin, language of the learned, but in the vulgar tongue of the Spanish people. Such proactive thinking measured by Alfonso was seen by historians as wise and appropriate to his sobriquet, *el Sabio*. With the king's backing, the region of Castile had become a learning center and a cultural mix of scholars and lay people amidst the milieu of Jewish, Muslim and Christian tradition[s]. The Arab original, the *Ghāyat Al-Ḥakīm*, "The Goal of the Wise," represents a medieval work on the subject of Astrology. According to Hashem Atallah, "The *Ghayat Al-Hakim* is a philosophical

---

[18] Bakhouche et al., *Picatrix*, 23-24.

work as well as one concerning astrology" (*Picatrix*, xii).[19] But the Latin
Picatrix is more than just a translation, as the Arabic text, itself a
compilation of classical and Arabic sources, has been expanded by the
translator as translators. The importance of the *Picatrix* during the thirteenth
century was large, and though its importance gradually waned in subsequent
centuries, the sixteenth century, "revived" its importance. What is more, as
William Kiesel notes, "With such colorful figures surrounding the Picatrix,
it is no wonder that scholars such as Lynn Thorndike and Frances A. Yates
would dedicate many pages to it" (xvi); these figures included the likes of
Marsilio Ficino, Pico della Mirandola, Peter of Abano and Henry Cornelius
Agrippa who received the *Picatrix* with open arms. Further, with the
influences of Aristotle and Plato, as well as the Nabateans, even a Latin
translation made its way into the hands of the Bard Rabelais; hence, the
Picatrix suggested an intriguing and *super*natural appeal to a wide audience,
establishing it as, arguably, a transcendent text of science and magic. In its
opening chapter, the *Picatrix* links the subject of wisdom with virtue, a
positioning reminiscent of Aristotelian and later a reaffirming Isidoran
idealism. The author opens chapter one of the first book as follows:

> Scias, o frater carissime, quod maius donum et nobilius quod Deus
> hominibus huius mundi dederit est scire quia per scire habetur noticia de
> rebus antiquis et que sunt cause omnium rerum huius mundi [...] et propter
> hoc sciuntur omnia que sunt et qualiter sunt, et qualiter una res post aliam in
> ordine elevatur, et in quo loco ille qui est radix et principium omnium huius
> mundi rerum existit, et per eum omnia dissolvuntur, et per ipsum omnia
> nova et vetera sciuntur (3).[20]

> Know, most dear brother, that the greatest and noblest gift which God has
> given to the people of this world is to know things, because through knowing

---

[19] This is an English translation of the first two books of the Arabic text: *Picatrix*
[*Ghayat Al-Hakim*]: *The Goal of the Wise*, trans. Hashem Atallah, ed., William
Kiesel, volume 1 (Seattle: Ourboros Press, 2002). There is no English translation of
the Spanish or Latin versions, although a French translation of the latter has been
completed by Bakhouche et. al., based on the Latin text presented in *Picatrix: The
Latin Version of the Ghāyat Al-Ḥakīm*, ed. David Pingree, Studies of the Warburg
Institute 39 (London: Warburg Institiute, 1986). Pingree has established that the Latin
text is a faithful translation of the Spanish. The Spanish translation of Marrelino
Villegas, Abul-Casim Maslama Ben Ahmad, *Picatrix: El fin del Sabio y el Mejor de
los dos medios para avanzar* (Madrid: Editoria Nacional, 1982), is a translation of
the Arabic text published by Hellmut Ritter as *Ghayat al-hakim wa-ahaqq al-
natijatayn bi-aitaqdim = Das Ziel des Weisen*, Studien der Bibliothek Warberg, 12
(Berlin: Teubner, 1933) (29).
[20] All the Latin quotations from the *Picatrix* are taken from David Pingree's edition.

one has awareness of ancient things which are the causes of all the things of the world [...] and by this all things which exist are known and of what manner they are, and in what manner one thing ascends in order after another, and in what place arises that which is the root and principle of all the things in our world, and through which all things are dissolved, and through which are known all things new and ancient.

The author continues to challenge and admonish all the while reminding the reader that God is the prime mover and different from all other things: "Ipse vero non est corpus nec ex aliquot corpore compositus," ("Himself [God] however is not a body nor composed from any kind of body"), and again that he "nec est mixtus cum aliquo alio extra sed totus est in se ipso" ("is not mixed with anything else from without, but is complete in himself") (3). The author of the *Picatrix* is keen to alert his readership of the position God holds in comparison to anything, or anyone else. After all, "ipse est prima veritas nec alterius indiget veritate" ("He himself is the prime truth, nor does He need the truth of anything else") (3). In continuing the conversation the author suggests that to know things is "res summa et nobilis" ("a thing supreme and noble") and that "quotidie studere debes in Deo — scilicet in mandates ipsius atque in bonitate eius — quia scientia, sensus et bonitas ab ipso procedunt" ("you ought to study every day in God—that is to say in his injunctions and in his goodness—because knowledge, understanding and goodness proceed from him" (4). The chapter then concludes as it begins:

> Et hoc est maximum donum quod ipse Deus hominibus dedit, ut studeant scire et cognoscere. Nam studere servire Deus est. Et nota quod scire tres proprietates habet, quarum prima est quod semper acquirit et numquam minuit, secunda quod semper elevatur et numquam degradatur, tercia quod semper apparet et numquam se abscondit (4).

> And it is the greatest gift that God has given to people that they apply themselves to knowing things and understanding them. For to know things is to serve God. And note that to the knowing of things has three properties: of which the first is that one always adds to it and never diminishes it; the second is that it is always it is raised up and never degraded; the third is to always shows itself and never conceals itself.

In Chapter 2 of the *Picatrix*, the author opens with a definition of magic, and classifies those who are able to understand its craft from those who cannot. The author asserts:

> Scias quod ista sciencia nominatur nigromancia. Nigromanciam appellamus omnia que homo operatur et ex quibus sensus et spiritus sequuntur illo opere

per omnes partes et pro rebus mirabilibus quibus operantur quod sensus
sequatur ea admeditando vel admirando (5).

Know that this knowledge is called nigromancy. We call nigromancy all that
someone works at and from which understanding and inspiration (spirit)
follow from that task throughout all its parts, and on account of the
wonderful things which follow what the understanding does by meditating
on or admiring it.

And this knowledge, "nimis est profunda et fortis intellectui," ("is
extraordinarily profound and tough in understanding" (5). Part of this
science is practical because its operations are "de spiritu in spiritum,"
("concerning a spirit in a spirit") (5). Among the practical aspects of this
science is the use of the talismans. "Et ymaginum composicio est spritus in
corpore, et composicio alchemie est corpus in corpore," ("And the
composition of a talisman is spirit in matter, and the composition of alchemy
matter in matter" (5). The author continues: "Et generaliter nigromanciam
dicimus pro omnibus rebus absconditis a sensu et quas maior pars hominum
non apprehendit quomodo fiant nec quibus de causis veniant," ("And
generally we speak of nigromancy with regard to all things hidden from the
understanding and which the majority of people do not comprehend how
they come into being nor from what causes they come") (5). The position of
the talisman in some manner makes sense of the "beyond" that is attached to
a comprehension of magic. Seemingly, this fact in which science provides
an answer at all, may assist in the parallel of magic and astrology, or better
still—the existence of knowledge via magic as science. In keeping with
Garrosa Resina's earlier remarks regarding magic as coercion, the *Picatrix*,
admittedly, echoes such a stance. The author suggests:

Et ymagines sapientes appellant telsam, quod interpretatur violator quia
quicquid facit ymago per violenciam facit et pro vincendo facit illud pro quo
est composite. Pro opera victorie facit proporcionibus arismetricis et
influenciis atque celestibus operibus (5).

And wise people call talismans *telsam*, which is interpreted as "violator"
because everything the talisman does, it acts through violence and it acts in
that way in order to conquer that for which it is made. For the achievement
of victory, it acts according to the proportions of arithmetic and the
emanations from the stars and the operations of the heavenly bodies.

Markedly, the use of numerology, assisted by mathematical semiotics
embedded within the "art" of Astrology, places "magic" in some modicum
of illumination with regards to the "knowing" of one's station; further, the
belief system which surrounds this idea is couched in a much larger sphere

of understanding where experimental science, or early chemistry can be identified. The author isolates such experimental science as alchemy when he compares the talisman to the elixir:

> Et similiter elixir idem in alchimia facit quia leviter convertit corpora de una natura in aliam nobiliorem, primo cooperienda spiritum, duriciem et stridorem, et tollendo sonum et sordiciem. Et istud est secretum elixir secundum sapientes antiquos. Et hoc nomen elixir interpretatur fortitude que alias fortidudines frangit convincendo et transmutat de una proprietate ad aliam quousque reducit eam ad sui similitudinem (5).

> And in a similar way the elixir does the same alchemically, because it easily changes substances from one nature into another, more noble, first overwhelming the spirit, the hardness, and the shrillness and removing the noise and the impurity. And this is the secret of the elixir according to wise people of old. The name elixir is interpreted as a strength which breaks other strengths overcoming them and transmutes them from one property to another until it reduces it to its own likeness.

Such reversals are contextual and though these "states" are dynamic in their alteration, the *Picatrix* posits the position of magic as a two-fold existence; first, magic is theoretical; second, magic is practical:

> Et dico quod nigromancia dividitur in duas partes, scilicet in theoricam et practicam. Theorica est sciencia locorum stellarum fixarum, quia ex eis componuntur celestes figure et forme celi. [...] Practica vero est composicio trium naturarum cum virtute infusionis stellarum fixarum (6).

> And I say that nigromancy is divided into two parts, that is into a theoretical and a practical. The theoretical is the knowledge of the positions of the fixed stars, because from them are devised the heavenly figures and the configurations of the heaven [...] The practical however is the combination of three natures [animal, vegetable, mineral] with the power of the infusion of the fixed stars.

A Rhetoric of Magic here revolves, or rather involves the subject of knowledge, that is, "science"; specifically, it pertains to the craft of Astrology. *Nigromancy* is without a doubt connected with science as the succeeding chapters demonstrate. Chapter three deals with the nature of the heavens and its matter (54-55); chapter four with the general positions and configurations of the heavens in order to make talismans (54-63); chapter five, examples of these positions and why one has need of them in order to make talismans (64-78); chapter six, in what degree everyone is in the world and how one knows that man is a microcosm reflecting a macrocosm (79-83); and book one concludes with chapter seven, in what degree one

finds each thing in the world, and other secrets, numerous, profound, hidden
by the sages and which we propose to reveal in this book.

Book two is concerned with astronomical matters, especially the
importance of the eighth or fixed sphere and why this is important for the
"science of talismans" (87-173); Book three deals with the properties of the
planets and the signs of the Zodiac (175-292); Book four deals with the
properties of spirits and how one is assisted in this art with talismans,
fumigations (incense) and other things. It concludes with a description of
talismans which expose admirable powers found in a book discussed in the
Church at Córdoba (293-378). Such an important text proved valuable in the
progressive formation of Spanish intellectual history, especially under the
auspices of Alfonso X.

2.3 Alfonso X, el Sabio: Life, Las Siete Partidas
and el Lapidario

Alfonso X (1221-1284) is known as *el Sabio* because of his rigorous
attempts to bring Spain into an informed, cultural sphere of learning. This
was accomplished through Alfonos's extensive literary activities and in
particular his adoption of Roman Civil Law to thirteenth century Spain in
Las Siete Partidas (herein, *Partidas*).[21] Again, justice was the king's
concern. For this project we will examine selections from Alfonso's
Partidas and his *Lapidario*, and the impact such literature may have
revealed during the thirteenth century; arguably, such texts seem to have
added to a growing Medieval Spanish intellectual history, but first let us
examine Alfonso X and his court.

Alfonso X was king of Castile-León in the third quarter of his life and
held great interest in many intellectual pursuits and participated in many
academic exercises. As one critic has noted, "He had many scholars in his
traveling court, and he was an active participant in their writing and editing."
Further, Alfonso aligned himself with those scholars who were well-versed
on Roman law, which prepared the king for his understanding to assemble a
uniform code for his lands. The work—known as *Las Siete Partidas*, or the
"Seven-Part Code" was in part responsible for an ethic of behavior
describing the way the human future should look like, as opposed to the

---

[21] Alfonso's *Siete Partidas* was compiled 1256-65 and was originally known as the
Libro de las Leyes, or the *Fuero de las Leyes*; moreover, the work was finally revised
by jurists of the fourteenth century and called *Las Siete Partidas* or *Leyes de
Partidas*. I will refer to this latter label for this current project.

behavior described in the *Chronicles*.[22] Among his other important works are his *Crónica General,* a history of Spain from the beginnings to the thirteenth century, and the *Grande y General Estoria,* an incomplete attempt to describe his history of the world from creation to the time of St. Anne. Further, Alfonso X compiled a *Lapidario,* a *Libro de las Formas y Imagenes* and a book on Astrology, *El Libro Cumplido en los Indizios de las Estrellas.* His own literary output consists of poems to the Virgin Mary: *Cantigas de Santa María.* Still, how is it exactly that such a king and his court was able to write in the vernacular tongue and privilege its syntax as a worthy language of intelligent and discursive, literary form?

Historically, the scholars that were invited to the court of Alfonso X, wrote in the Castilian tongue, and by regularizing the syntax, made in the process a literary language. The *Partidas* as we have already mentioned were in part based on Roman Civil Law, and provided codes on manners, morals, the concept of the king and his people as an *universitas,* or union (corporation of sorts), within which the king existed as agent of both God and the people. Enduring a Moorish uprising in 1264, Alfonso, stimulated his cultural *vita* in the latter part of the thirteenth century, relying on *l'histoire commander son passé.* Although he may have been considered learned, wise, and to some extent a progressive intellectual, Alfonso was a poor politician; his focus on learning was unquestionable, but his ambitions to become Holy Roman Emperor were too self-seeking and locally, counter-

---

[22] *Las Siete Partidas* according to the Medieval Sourcebook taken from http://origin.web.fordham.edu/halsall/source/jews-sietepart.html: 15 June 2007

   Is one of the most remarkable law codes of medieval times. The code, written in the Castilian vernacular, was compiled about 1265, under the supervision of Alfonso X, the Wise (1252-1284), of Castile. Its laws, however, did not go into effect until 1348, and then only with certain reservations. From Castile they spread to all of Spain and thence into the Spanish possessions in the Philippines, Porto Rico, Florida, and Louisiana. The sources of this code are largely Visigothic, later Roman, and Church law, all of which were hostile to the Jew. This hostility did not, however, deter the Castilian state from protecting scrupulously the Jewish religion as well as the person and property of the Jews. The Jews and Moors, national minorities, were too numerous and too important to be mistreated as yet by the new Castilian state.

What is of considerable interest here is the importance of such alterity as it concerns the Jews for their intellectual translating ability and the information they wielded. Alfonso not only recognized, but proactively attempted to protect such a resource as national, intellectual capital to the furtherance of an educated and better-informed Spain.

intuitive with respect to any national unification.[23] He advanced the existing
schools of both Seville and Salamanca, and provided a tolerant atmosphere
for both Muslim and Jewish cultural existence. Such cultural *tolerance* did
not last as the pogroms of 1391 demonstrate. In Castille the laws of 1412
confined Jews to ghettos and regulated their dress. Similar legislation was
passed in Aragon, and the final expulsion of the Jews came in 1492—
beginning with the *Edict of Expulsion of the Jews*, 29 April 1492. George D.
Greenia in her review of, *"The Lapidary of King Alfonso X the Learned* by
Ingrid Bahler" suggests, "Alfonso X was certainly one of the great monarchs
of his age and an independent scholar who enjoyed the means to turn the
fruits of his research pastimes into luxury objects of conspicuous
consumption" (791).[24] Regardless of Alfonso's motives for spreading
knowledge and the "texture of the medieval world, where concrete reality
and fantasy have equal standing and mix freely," Greenia reaffirms, rather
than discredits, such a time period in which the ambiguities of belief and
belief systems (including magic) were able to co-exist. What is more, the
more detailed an explanation of the supernatural there was, the less credible
it seemed.[25] Alfonso's interests as king and curious intellectual went hand-
in-hand, and his support of Arabic translations into Castilian was to him a
worthwhile investment. The *Lapidario* is a good example of such a work
based on classical sources. It contains a list of almost 500 stones, each with
accompanying signs of the zodiac, assorted stars, letters of the alphabet and
other "pertinent" information. Further, it relies on Ptolemy's astrological

---

[23] Marie R. Madden's *Political Theory and Law in Medieval Spain* (New York:
Fordham University Press, 1930), suggests a tolerant backdrop for Spain. Madden
asserts:

> As the Spanish power recovered in its struggle against the Moorish
> invasions, towns became populated, new towns were formed and country
> districts were settled. With the conquered Moors and the conquering
> Spaniards taking up peaceful relations, trade and agriculture flourished. (65)

[24] *Hispania*, 83.4 (Dec., 2000), 791-92.

[25] In referencing the subject of magic and its forms to excite and inform the senses
Valerie I. J. Flint provides a definition of sorts in *The Rise of Magic in Early
Medieval Europe* (Princeton: Princeton University Press, 1991). Flint asserts that,
"Magic may be said to be the exercise of preternatural control over nature by human
beings, with the assistance of forces more powerful than they," and again that
"Sometimes, of course, *magic* is employed as a term of abuse: but at least as often, I
would contend, it is used to describe a type of excitement, or wonder, or sudden
delight, that is not proper but without which life might be seriously the poorer" (3).
Here then magic has taken on a cultural role imbued in the lives of the everyday
phenomena, and for this purpose as we shall note, Alfonso and his court play a vital
role in its *regulation*.

treatise, the *Almagest*. Alfonso had also created his own astronomical texts and charts based on the meridian of Toledo. Greenia asserts:

> The scientific lore of the Middle Ages is all too often bypassed now as foolish speculation, yet it has a great deal to teach us about the conscientious systematization of natural history, the conceptual architecture that supported a sophisticated world view, and the continuity of natural white magic (including geology, medicine, astrology and casting horoscopes) with black magic and demonology. (791)

Such an analysis suggests that Alfonso X, though conflating myth and fact and knotting together astrology and folklore, may have still produced or rather, commissioned, "smartly commodified cultural goods that would impress both his unlettered countrymen and learned diplomats from abroad" (791). Here, the king privileges his role as educator of his eclectic people (Christians, Muslims and Jews), and applies such intellectual energy toward the fashioning of his *Lapidario*.

The *Lapidario* of Alfonso X which was begun in 1250 and completed in 1270, opens with "Del Signo De Aries," ["The sign of Aries"] (*Lapidario* 13) and involves the "piedra a que llaman magnitat en caldeo y en arabigo, y en latin magnetes, y en lenguaje castellano aymant," ["rock or stone called magnitat in Chaldean and in Arabic, and in Latin *magnetes*, and in the Castillian tongue Imán"] (13). Moreover, the remainder of the text is sectioned by the remaining 11 zodiac signs. There are too many stones to list which have properties than can heal, kill, provide the love, or the lust of a woman, produce good[s] or *maleficium*.[26] Comparatively, Alfonso links each stone with a specific star and zodiac sign plus number, and temperature. For example, the stone that is called *çurudica*, which he translates as pertaining to the liver and appears "cárden en su color," ["purple in color or hue"] (15), is hot and dry to the touch "y segun

---

[26] The layout of the *Lapidario* is taken from the edition prepared by María Brey Mariño (*Alfonso X, Rey de Castilla: Lapidario*, Madrid: Editorial Castalia, 1968); further, the text opens with an outline of figures of the constellations; a prologue which warns that he who would enjoy the fullness of the wisdom found within the pages of this book, "que sea sabidor de astronomia," ["that he be knowledgeable concerning the works of astrology"] (11); moreover, each zodiac sign is mentioned, and within each zodiac sign the stones that pertain to that zodiac sign. For example, the sign that is associated with Aries contains 31 chapter sections with each section detailing a particular characteristic of a stone (hence, 31 stones); i.e. its power or influence, its heat, its qualities ranging from *beneficum* to *maleficium* as well as its association to other stars. This prescriptive methodology continues from Aries with: Taurus, Gemini, Cancer, Leo, Virgo, Libra, Scorpion, Sagittarius, Capricorn, Aquarius, and Pisces (13-231).

naturaleza de fisica para obrar mal," ["and given its natural, physical state will cause harm"] (15). The stone is associated with "La estrella mediana de las tres que estan en la cinta de la Mujer Ecadenada," ["the medium sized star of the three that is located at the skirt or tape of the Woman in Chains"] (123).[27] Of the stone called *mármol*, ["marble"] Alfonso asserts it has the properties to "hace gran bien," or do "great good" and that moreover such a stone "tiene poder," or "has power" if mixed with "cera," or "wax" and "aceite," or "oil" to grant both "la fuerza y la virtud," or "great strength and virtue" (123). This stone is to be ground and boiled in water over a fire. A final example employs the use of a nameless stone that "arranca las uñas," or "rips out one's fingernails" (122). In the *Lapidario*, Alfonso is clear about which stones harm, or are *Maléficas* (*Maleficios*) and should not be approached with impunity. Some stones appeared only at specific moments of planetary alignments and in the sea; one such example is a stone associated with Saturn and the sign of Aquarius. It is only discovered when the sea is heavily undulated, tumultuous and unsettled. Alfonso notes, "Hay en ella una virtud muy mala: que si la mira alguno cuando Saturno esta bajo tierra, ciega, y mirandola mientras esta la estrella sobre tierra, no hace mal," ["There is in this stone a very harmful power: that if someone should look at it while Saturn is under the Earth, is blinded, and observing it [the stone] when the star is above the Earth, no harm will come"] (224). Such belief in the rising and setting of planets dictated a symbiotic link to one's birth and Saturn is held, in astrological terms, as a planetary birth charter. Though the *Lapidario* provides a look into the scholarly interest regarding Astrology and Astronomy, Alfonso X took it upon himself to extend such academic and intellectual zeal into a codified representation for a civil Spanish society. The emergence of *Las Siete Partidas* is the result of such attempted "codification."

In his massive *Las Siete Partidas* (c.a.1256-65; herein, *Partidas*), an attempt at literary exchange involving a code of manners and socio-political synergy, albeit a biased one as we shall soon note, Alfonso X in title I to his first *Partida* opens with:

> A Servicio de Dios, e a pro communal delas gentes fazemos este libro, segun q*ue* mostramos enel comienço del. E partimos lo en siete partes, en la manera que diximos de suso: porq*ue* los que leyessen, fallassen ay todas las cosas cu*m*plidas, e ciertas, para aprovechar se dellas. (I.3ʳ)[28]

---

[27] The "Chained Maiden" in Astrology is the constellation Andromeda.

[28] For the Spanish quotations from Alfonso X's *Partidas* I have relied on a three volume reprint of the Gregorio López edition of 1555 which is legally the

> We make this book for the service of God and the common benefit of nations, as we have shown in its beginning. And we divide it into Seven Parts, in the manner which we have mentioned above, in order that those who read it may find therein all things complete and certain, in order to be able to profit by them.

And so begins the opening to the first volume or *Partida*, which is comprised of XXIV *Titulos*, or "titles;" each title contains varying numbers of laws. The first three titles concern themselves with what the laws are, in what manner and manners are these laws to be observed beginning with the Holy Trinity and the Catholic Faith. The first *Partida* deals with Church doctrine as well as the behavior of the clergy and the structure and the democracy of Church hierarchy. The second *Partida* concerns the king's behavior and his ability to add laws. In this sense the king is not above the statutes, but surely not beneath them. What concerns us here is how the community or people are to behave accordingly and civilly with one another; these are to be found in *Partida* II, titles XII-XIII respectively. In this second *Partida* then Alfonso continues to engage in the issue of war and how to handle one's enemies, or prisoners of war (POWs), while *Partida* III deals with legal procedures, the roles of lawyers, oaths, evidence, judgment, concluding with property and possession. The fourth *Partida* deals with family laws, slavery and vassalage and the fifth *Partida* deals with commercial and maritime law. The sixth *Partida* deals with the laws of inheritance while the final and seventh *Partida* concerns crime and criminals, sexual transgressions, magic, those in adultery, then: the Jews, the Moors, heretics and blasphemers. The final *Partida* concludes with titles on prisons, torture, and punishment while the 34th title lists 37 rules or maxims necessary for the successful conduct of the Law. This brief overview surveys Alfonso X's vast mind concerning the central focus of an informed, thirteenth century medieval community, and aids in the cementing of a Medieval Spanish intellectual history.

In the first *Partida*, Alfonso suggests in title I, law LXVI "Como son todos tenudos de guardar las leyes," ["Why All Persons Are Required to Observe the Laws"] (I: 8ᵛ). Alfonso exaplains:

---

authoritative text: *Las Siete Partidas*, ed. Gregorio López. (Salamanca: Andrea de Portoais, 1555), reprint in 3 vols. (Madrid: Boletin Oficial del Estado, 1974). Since each Partida is separately foliated, the Spanish quotations will be identified by Partida number and the appropriate folio, *recto* or *verso*. There is a complete English translation of the López edition, *Las Siete Partidas*, trans, Samuel Parson Scott, ed. Robert F. Burns, S.J., 5 vols. (Philadelphia: University of Pennsylvania Press, 2001), from which the English translations are taken. All five volumes are continually paginated and citations will be to volume and page numbers.

Guarder deve el rey las leyes como asu honrra e a su fechura, porque recibe poder e razon para fazer justicia [...] E otrosi, las deve guardar el pueblo, como a su vida e a su pro: porque por ellas bive*n* en paz, e resciben plazer e proveccho de lo q*ue* an. (I: 8^v-9^r)

The king should observe the laws as he would his honor and his handiwork, because he is endowed with power and reason in order to dispense justice [...] On the other hand, the people should observe the laws as they would their lives and their well being: because by means of them they live in peace and receive pleasure and profit from their possessions. (I: 6)

In Chapter 1, we examined the powerful use[s] of language and semantics as well as Stuart Clark's Rhetoric of Witchcraft and the influence such claims held toward the aristocracy. Here, we note that the language of the law rules over temporal matters and sustains order from the king down toward the common people. Alfonso was not only particularly concerned with the power of speech and language rules, but also with justice and order, and insisted that each member of society contribute to such an order. Moreover, such an ordering of earthly hierarchy was a reflection of the heavenly structure, wherein God is head and everything else distends from Him. In the introduction to title III, Alfonso comments on the Holy Trinity as well as on the Articles of the Catholic Faith. He asserts:

Començamiento de las leyes, tambien de las temporales como de las spirituales, es esto: q*ue* todo Christiano crea firmame*n*te, q*ue* es un solo verdadero Dios, que no*n* ha comienço, ni fin, ni ha en si medida, ni mudamiento, e es poderoso sobre todas las cosas, seso de ome non puede entender, ni fablar del cumplidamente, padre, e fijo, e Spiritu santo, tres personas, e una cosa simple, sin departimiento, que es Dios padre, non fecho, ni engendrado de otro. (I: 13^v-14^r)

The origin of laws, temporal as well as spiritual, is this, that every Christian should believe firmly that there is one true God who has neither beginning nor end, who is neither subject to limitation nor change, and has power over all things, and that the brain of man cannot understand or describe Him perfectly; and that Father, Son, and holy Spirit are three persons and one thing, simple, without division, which is God the Father, neither created nor begotten by another. (I: 14)

Those who did not adhere to such tenets of the Faith were deemed heretic, and deserved, in addition to God's wrath, a more temporal punishment; such penalties involved death and forced conversion.[29] The

---

[29] In Joseph O'Callaghan's *The Learned King: The Reign of Alfonso X of Castile*, (Philadelphia: University of Pennsylvania Press, 1993) he asserts, "The penalty for

focus then of the later laws within subsequent sections of the *Partidas* provided an answer to such a contentious challenge and administered its response with vehement, religious flame.

In observing the explanation of phenomena, Alfonso articulates his position via the differences that exist between *naturalis* and *miraculum*. This idea is to be found within the first *Partida*, title IV, law LXVII as Alfonso states:

> Natura es fechura de Dios, e el es el señor e el fazedor della. Onde todo lo q*ue* pue de ser fecho por natura, faze Dios, e de mas otras cosas a que non cumple el poder de la natura: ca la natura non puede dexar, nin desviarse de obrar, segund la orden cierta que puso Dios porq*ue* obrasse, as si como fazer noche, dia, e frio e calentura: otrosi, q*ue* los tie*m*pos no*n* recuda*n* a sus sazones, segu*n*d el movimie*n*to cierto del cielo, e delas estrellas, en quie*n* puso Dios virtud e poder de ordenar la natura. (I: 31^v)

> Nature is the act of God, and he is the Lord and maker of it, for God does all that can be done by Nature, and other things besides which the power of Nature cannot effect; for Nature cannot cease, or turn aside from action according to the positive regulation which God imposed upon it; as, for instance, to produce night and day, cold and heat, and also to prevent the seasons from failing to return at their proper times, according to the certain motions of heaven and the stars, upon which God conferred the virtue and power of regulating Nature. (I: 45)

Could this regulating of Nature suggest a good use for mandating order in the world itself? It is, after all, as we have noted via Alfonsan dictation, a realm ruled by the triune God. Again, this parallels our earlier concerns regarding the source or wellspring of such ability to explain phenomena; consider, that where the source is God and Divine agency, the resulting phenomena is categorized as *miraculum*; in the event that an opposing source, or force is utilized and considered hostile to the Divine parameters, the law of contraries suggests its opposite—the Devil is responsible, and as such the dark arts are manifested and utilized via Satanas and *maleficium*. Of course, difficulty arises when both elements conflate and their source of power is ambiguous, if not, deficient of any clear distinction. Further, what

---

heresy, and also for those converting from Christianity to Judaism or Islam, was death by fire" (49). Morevoer, O'Callaghan posits that "In the twelfth and thirteenth centuries the kings of Castile-León consistently portrayed themselves as faithful sons of the Church," and that specifically Alfonso X, "presented himself to the world as a dutiful Christian, concerned about the maintenance of religious orthodoxy and the well-being of the church" (49). See Partida VII, title XXVI, law 2: "el herege…deven lo quemar en fuego" (3: 79) ("the heretic…should be put to death by fire" [V: 1443]).

are we to do when the formation of phenomena is explained *ex nihilo*, out of
nothing? In explaining the position of miracle[s] and the ability to create *ex
nihilo*, Alfonso suggests in *Partida* I, title IV, law LXVII:

> [E] este poder es apartadamente de Dios: e quando obra por el, alo que faze
> dizen le miraglo, porque quando acaesce, es cosa maravillosa a los omes, e
> las gentes […] Ca estonce han fe de maravillar como de cosa nueva e
> estraña, e desta fablo e con razon, dixo, Miraglo es cosa que veemos, mas
> non sabemos onde viene: esto se entiende quanto al pueblo comunalmente.
> Mas los sabios e los entendidos bien entienden, que la cosa que non puede
> fazer natura, nin artificio del ome que del poder de Dios viene tan solamente,
> e non de otro. (I: 31^v-32^r)

> This power is peculiarly that of God, and when it is manifestad by Him the
> act is called a miracle, because when it happens it is a marvelous thing both
> to men and nations […] for then they [the observing nations] marvel at it as
> something new and strange; and of this the wise man spoke, and with reason
> said; "A miracle is something which we see but do not know when it
> comes." This is understood to apply to the people in general, but wise men
> and educated persons well understand that anything that Nature cannot do, or
> the skill of man accomplish, is derived solely from the power of God and
> from no other source. (I: 46)

What is more, Alfonso continues his explanation of *miracula* into the
following law LXVIII, but notes that miracles are not frequent and must
come through the power of God, and not through *arte*, or "craft". Lastly,
such phenomena is to hold no higher purpose than "que aquel miraglo
acaesca, sobre cosa que sea sobre confirmacion de la fe," ["the miracle must
relate to something which may tend to the confirmation of the Faith"] (I: 32^r;
I: 46). The keeping of the Faith occupied the attention of Alfonso X, but
such a position, perhaps, was underscored when compared to the subject of
justice and the regulation for a better world. Recall, these laws or "codes"
were patterned after Roman Civil Law, which proposed the conduct of a
civil society amidst a myriad of cultures and belief[s], although the first
Partida, especially, has been heavily influenced by Canon Law.

In the third *Partida*, Alfonso is keen on examining the subject of justice
ranging from court disputes to the way it is applied via transactions between
men. He states in the introduction to title I:

> Justicia es una de las cosas, porque mejor e mas endreçamente se mantiene
> el mundo. E es assi como fuente onde manan todos los derechos. E non tan
> solamente ha logar Justicia en los pleytos que son entrelos demandadores e
> los demandados en juyzio: mas a un entre todas las otras cosas, que qui ên en
> entre avienen los omes quier se fagan por obra, o se digan por palabra. (III:
> 2^{r-v})

Justice is one of the things by means of which the World is better maintained and regulated. It is like a spring from whence all rights flow. And not only is justice employed in suits arising between plaintiffs and defendants in court, but also in all other transactions between men, whether they originate in deed or in word. (III: :534)

Of further interest is the manner in which Alfonso links Aristotelian idealism alongside the subject of justice. Alfonso is aware of the importance of justice and the benefits it affords, namely peaceful relations that sustain the world. We find this specifically in the third law under the first Titulo, wherein Alfonso suggests three "derechos," or rights:

El primero es, que ome biva honestamente, quanto en fi. El segundo, que non faga mal, nin daño a otro. El tercero, que de su derecho a cada uno. E aquel que cumple estos mandamientos faze lo que deve a Dios: e assi mismo, e a los omes con quien bive, e cumple, e mantiene la Justicia. (III: 3ʳ)

[F]irst, that every man should live honestly, so far as he himself is concerned; second, that he should not do wrong or injury to another; third, that he should give to each one that to which he is entitled. He who complies with these precepts performs his duty to God, to himself and to the men with whom he lives, and renders and maintains justice. (III: 535)

From an initial definition of justice and its benefits Alfonso continues to distill in a prescriptive manner the elements that are related to justice; i.e., the subject of the "demandante," or plaintiff, the "demandado," or defendant, judges, "abogados," or attorneys, the summons, the subject of proof and witnesses, and that of judgments and appeals and clemency. This non-exhaustive list is but a reflection of a grand, learned mind and a king's desire to have an informed and responsible community.

We will by-pass now *Partidas* Four through Six, which concern such varied topics as family law and social relations, property and commercial law, and wills and inheritances and will examine, rather closely, the seventh *Partida* concerning: "todas las acusaciones, e maleficios que los omes fazen, e que pena me rescen aver porende," ["all the accusations and offenses which men commit and what punishment they deserve therefore"] (VII: 2ʳ; V: 1303).

Alfonso X begins with a charge and a warning regarding the adherence of things past, namely those "things" which cause men to err, and to be vigilant for them that behave in such a reprobate conduct. In titles I through XXII he is concerned with accusations, treason and false witnesses, trial by combat, loss of stature, infamy, deception and false measures, homicide, violence and repudiation of friendships, truce and security, theft, fraud, adultery (of which he knew something about, because he had four illegitimate children), sexual malpractice[s], seduction and even sodomy. By providing his community and his court with the wherewithal to live in the midst of such behavior and practices, Alfonso ensured that a civil society, equal to a godly one, would not live in ignorance. Still, we are interested however in Alfonso X's position on the subject of necromancy and divination, as well as his stance on the Jews and Moors, and the characteristics of Heresy.

Previously, we have considered the subtle definitions and distinctions between necromancy and *nigromancia*, two practices concerning the subject of magic; the former has never been associated in the positive light, and the latter, a bit of a pun on the dark, or "black" arts, is always seen in a more, darker vein. In the seventh *Partida* Alfonso is concerned with making the community aware of necromantic practices and their derivative affectations that involve divination—itself a form of magic. These practitioners he [Alfonso] categorizes as heretics, and as such is concerned with those *agents* of such belief and belief systems in the Christian community; moreover, Alphonso is specifically concerned with their [heretics] attempt to ascertain the future from a two-fold methodology; the first involves that art of which we have made mention of before, namely Astrology; the second, participates in the acts of magic, sooth-saying, fortune-telling, and even theurgy. He picks up the topic in title XXIII in which the introduction matter-of-factly claims:

> A Devinar las cosas que han de venir cobdician los omes naturalmente, e por que algu*n*os dellos pruevan esto en muchas maneras yerran ellos, e ponen otros muchos algue*n*os en yerro […] E demostraremos q*ue* quiere decir adevinança. E qua*n*tas maneras son della. E ante quie*n* puede ser dema*n*dada. E que pena merece*n*, los que se trabajan, a obrar della, como non deven. (VII: 73ᵛ)

> Men naturally desire to ascertain coming events, and because some of them attempt this by numerous methods, they are guilty of sin and induce many others to do wrong […] We shall show what divination means; how many kinds there are; who can accuse parties who are guilty of it; before whom such an offense can be prosecuted; and what penalty those deserve who attempt to practice it as they should not do. (V: 1431)

Alfonso is aware that such behaviors are aberrant to the Church and what is more, that these agents err toward his goal of a civil union because they, these *practitioners*, disturb the waters of just cause and *paz*, or peace. We shall note, however, where such practices via the agency of Divine influence, can be utilized for the good of the masses, or in Alfonso's case, the court and his people. This "good" is what he refers to as benefits and profits, as we have already noted. Still, Alfonso is keen to denounce such practices as they do not serve a purpose within his greater plan. In law I, "Que cosa es adevinança: e quantas maneras son della," ["What Divination Is, and How Many Kinds There Are"], Alfonso states:

> ADevinança tanto quiere dezir como querer tomar el poder de Dios para saber las cosas que estan por venir. E son dos maneras de adevinança. La primera es la que se faze por arte de Astronomia, que es, una de las siete artes liberales, esta segund el fuero de las leyes non es defendida de usar a los que son maestros, e la entienden verdaderamente: por que los juyzios, e los asmamientos que se dan por esta arte, son catados por el curso natural, de las planetas e de las otras estrellas: e fueron tomadas, de los libros de Ptolomeo, e do los otros sabidores: que se trabajaron de esta sciencia. (VII: 73^v)

> La segunda manera de adevinança es de los agoreros, e de los forteros, e de los fechizeros, que ca tan agueros de aves, o de estornudos, o de palabras a que llaman proverbio, o echan fuertes: o catan agua, o en cristal, o en espejo, o en espada, o en otra cosa luziente, o fazen fechuras de metal, o de otra cosa qualquier, o adevinança en cabeça de ome muerto, o de bestia o en palma de niño: o de muger virgen. E estos truhanes, e todos los otros semejantes dellos (por que son omes dañosos, e engañadores, e nascen desus fechos muy grandes males a la tierra) defendemos que ninguno dellos non more en nuestro señorio, nin use y destas cosas: e otrosi, que ninguno non sera osado delos acoger en sus casas, nin encubrirlos. (VII: 74^r)

Divination means the same thing as assuming the power of God in order to find out things which are to come. There are two kinds of divination, the first is, that which is accomplished by the aid of astronomy which is one of the seven liberal arts; and this, according to the law, is not forbidden to be practiced by those who are masters and understand it thoroughly; for the reason that the conclusions and estimates derived from this art are ascertained by the natural course of the planets and other stars, and are taken from the books of Ptolemy and other learned men, who diligently cultivated the science. (V: 1431)

The second kind of divination is that practiced by fortune-tellers, soothsayers, and magicians, who investigate omens caused by the flights of birds, by sneezing, and by words called proverbs; or by those who cast lots, or gaze in water, or in crystal, or in a mirror, or in the blade of a sword, or in any other bright object; or who make images of metal, or any other substance whatsoever; or practice divination on the head of a dead man, or that of an animal, or in the palm of a child, or that of a virgin. We forbid imposters of this kind and all others like them to live in our dominions, or practice any of these things here, because they are wicked and deceitful persons, and great evils result to the country from their acts; and we also forbid anyone to dare to entertain them in their houses, or conceal them. (V: 1431)

Alfonso makes the distinction that not all divination is bad or evil in its association; the divination that is associated with Astrology, however, must be accompanied by learned practitioners of the art. Why? Because it was held to be aligned with the "science" of that day and period, a thirteenth century justification that had imbedded within it the ancient wisdom of Ptolemy. Further, it was necessary to make the distinction between Astrology and fortune-telling, or what has become in our modern day, folk magic, or popular "street" magic. Alfonso continues to disassociate Astrology from other practices such as *necromantia*. He asserts in law II: "Necromantia dizen en latin, a un saber estraño que es para encantar espiritus malos, e por que de los omes que se trabajan a fazer esto, viene muy grand daño a la tierra [...] porende defendemos que ninguno non sea osado de se trabajar, nin de usar de tal enemiga como esta," ["What is called *necromatia*, in Latin, is the strange art of calling up evil spirits, and for the reason that great injury happens to the country [...] we therefore forbid that anyone shall dare to practice or make use of such wickedness as this"] (V: 1431). Seemingly, the damage that is to be done via such practice is not self-contained, but it leads the country into error, and a society in error disrupts the hope of a peaceful and civil society, albeit a society that never materialized within the lifetime of Alfonso X or his descendants. On the subject of magical herbs and potions that rendered the user under the "influence," Alfonso asserts:

> Otrosi defendemos que ninguno non sea osado de fazer ymagines decera, nin de metal, nin otros fechizos para enamorar los omes con las mugeres, nin para departir el amor que algunos oviessen entre si. E aun defendemos, que ninguno non sea osado de dar yeruas, nin brevaje a algund ome, nin a muger por razon de enamoramiento porq*ue* acaesce a las vegadas q*ue* destos brevajes vienen a muerte los omes que los toman, e han muy grandes enfermedades de que fincan ocasionados para siempre. (VII: 74^r)

> Moreover, we forbid anyone to do dare to make images of wax or metal, or any other figures to cause men to fall in love with women, or to put an end to the affection which persons entertain towards one another. We also forbid anyone to be so bold as to administer herbs or beverages to any man or woman to render them enamoured, because it sometimes happens that such beverages cause the death of those who take them, and they contract very serious diseases with which they are afflicted for life. (V: 1431-32)

The role of images and other means that allow the natural order, or state of the human species to alter toward the opposite or similar sex is for

Alfonso—forbidden. Again, those who would pursue such ends are deemed evil and are punished as heretics and suffer death; further, those who assist such peculiar behaviors are to be punished by permanent banishment from the realm. The ambiguity of such power, or influence, conversely, to Alfonso was always ambiguous depending upon the source or well-spring of the activity. What about the practitioner's intent—could it have any say at all in the matter regardless of the source of influence? Alfonso seems to think so and in fact suggests:

> Pero los que fiziessen encantamiento, o otras cosas, con entencion buena: assi como sacar demonios de los cuerpos de los omes o para desfligar a los que fuessen marido, e muger, que non pudiessen convenir, o para desatar nuve, que echasse granizo, o niebla, por que non corrompiesse los frutos: o para matar lagosta, o pulgon que daña el pan, o las viñas, o por alguna otra razon provechosa semejante destas, non deve aver pena: ante dezimos que deve recibir gualardon por ello. (VII: 74^r)

> Such, however, as practice enchantments or anything else with good intentions, as for instance, to cast out devils from the bodies of men; or to dissolve the spell cast over husband and wife so that they are unable to perform their marital duties; or to turn aside a cloud from which hail or a fog is descending, that it may not injure the crops; or to kill locusts or insects which destroy grain or vines; or for any other beneficial purpose similar to these cannot be punished, but we decree that they shall be rewarded for it. (V: 1432)

In short, the use of "magic" and its intention[s], or what I have suggested throughout this project as its "affectations," is commensurate with the practitioner's intent and motive; i.e. where harm and death ensue, *maleficium* is the terminus of such magic; subsequently, where "good" is to be profited, or gained from such an interaction of "positive" magic, *beneficium* is at stake. Both have their place in the ordering and understanding of one's world, and Alfonso supported such ideas as the aforementioned.[30] Alfonso, in commenting about the use[s] of "magic"

---

[30] Once more we rely on Flint's *The Rise of Magic in Early Medieval Europe* (Princeton: Princeton University Press, 1991), wherein she asserts, "I can only plead that *magic* is helpful as a sounding word for the exploration of the many in which a hopeful belief in preternatural control reached the early Middle Ages" (6). Magic is indeed helpful and as Alfonso, the Learned was aware, it needed to be defined, controlled and ultimately scapegoat[-ed] via the hegemonic labeling of all foreigners to the Iberian Peninsula. Further, Flint's assessment on magic and science as well as magic and religion are helpful when making distinctions between these parallels;

strongly suggested how "foreigners" ought to live amongst the *Spanish*. Most notably, we shall look at the Alfonsan view concerning both Jews and Moors followed by the defining and organizing against Heresy and its practitioner, namely that culpable outsider, the heretic.

In keeping with the other Great Christian Sovereigns, Alfonso X suggests a tolerance toward his Jewish neighbor[s] in hopes for a peaceful society. Alfonso suggests in title XXIV that, by definition, "Judios son una manera de gente que como quier que non creen la fe de nuestro señor Jesu Christo, pero los grandes señores de los Cristianos siempre sufrieron que biviessen entre ellos," ["Jews are a people who, although they do not believe in the religion of Our Lord Jesus Christ, yet, the great Christian sovereigns have always permitted them to live among them"] (VII: 74^v; V: 1433). Such a quasi-tolerance supported the claim that Spain proved to be, at least within this thirteenth century time period, a place of acceptance and lenience in the frame of recognition. Of further interest is how, Alfonso, in outlining how the Jewish populace is to live amongst the Christians, provides both a prescription and a warning of behavior. He asserts in law II of title XXIV:

> Mansamente: e sin mal bollicio deven fazer vida los judios entre los christianos guardando su ley, e non diziendo mal de la fe de nuestro señor jesu christo que guardan los cristianos. Otrosi se deven mucho guardarde predicar, ninconvertir ningun christiano, que se torne judio alabando su ley, e denostando la nuestra, E quel quier que contra esto fiziere deve morir porende, e perder lo que ha. (VII: 74^v)

> Jews should pass their lives among Christians quietly and without disorder, practicing their own religious rites, and not speaking ill of the truth of Our Lord Jesus Christ which Christians acknowledge. Moreover, a Jew should be very careful to avoid preaching to, or converting any Christian, to the end that he may become a Jew, by exalting his own belief and disparaging ours. Whoever violates this law shall be put to death and lose all his property. (V: 1433)

Strikingly, one might think this harsh treatment to be a non-tolerant approach to the co-habitant Jews; it should be noted, however, that they were allowed to continue their practices and rituals as pertaining to the Jewish tradition. They were given places to build their synagogues, a place of prayer and worship. Further, the Jews were given protection over such holy edifices, wherein Christians were told neither to deface the sanctuary nor to remove anything from within its walls. As pertaining to matters of

---

such parallels were explored in the first chapter. For further reading on the matter see Flint's *The Rise of Magic in Early Medieval Europe* chapters 3 and 5-respectively.

worship and the Sabbath day, or Saturday, no neighbor could bring railing accusation[s] to any Jewish neighbor because of their holy observance; this included no transaction involving the buying and selling of goods, the making of contracts, establishing the furtherance of business and even the collection of debts. Such levels of civility, however, had their place alongside that which Alfonso deemed heretical; for example, while there was to be no forced conversion of a Jew to Christianity, should Christians convert to Judaism, then they were to be condemned as heretics and burned and stripped of all their property. As history reminds us, this was just the beginning of a shift from "tolerance" to intolerance, which ultimately led to the expulsion of the Jews in 1492. If the existence of the Jews became perceived as an insult to the Christian community and their role as outsiders too much to bear, did the Moors (Muslims) fare any better?

The Moors are described by Alfonso in the introduction to title XXV as follows:

> Moros son una manera de gente, que creen que mahomat fue Propheta, e mandadero de Dios: e porque las obras que fizo non muestran del tan grand santidad, porque a tan santo estado pudiesse llegar, poren de la su ley es como de nuesto de Dios: Onde pues que...hablamos de los judios, e de la su ciega porfia que han contra la verdadera creencia: que remos aquí dezir de los moros, e de la su necedad, que creen. (VII: 76ᵛ)

> The Moors are a people who believe that Mohammed was the Prophet and Messenger of God, and for the reason that the works which he performed do not indicate the extraordinary sanctity which belongs to such a sacred calling, his religion is, as it were, an insult to God. Wherefore, since...we treated of the Jews and of the obstinacy which they display toward the true faith, we intend to speak here of the Moors, and of their foolish belief by which they think they will be saved. (V: 1438)

Alfonso is placing the Moors and their belief[s] on par with Jewish belief and *traditio*, and more importantly, linking the two with Heresy. Still, Alfonso, a champion of the Faith, felt it necessary to stipulate the co-habitation of Moors in Spain alongside Christians. He asserts:

> Sarracenus en latin tanto quiere dezir en romance como Moro: e tomo este nome de Sarra, que fue muger libre de Abrahan como quier que el linaje de los Moros non descendiesse della, mas de agar que fue servienta de Abrahan. E son dos maneras de Moros. La una es que non creen en el nuevo, nin el viejo testamento. E la otra es que rescibieron los cinco libros de Moysen, mas desecharon los Profetas, e non los quisieron creer. (VI: 76ᵛ)

> E dezimos que deven bivir los Moros entr los Christianos, en aquella mesmamanera, que diximos en el titulo ante deste que lo deven fazer los

judios guardando su ley, e no*n* denostando la nuestra. Pero en las villas delos Christinos non deven aver los Moros mezquitas, nin fazer sacrificio publicame*n*te ante los omes. E las mezquitas, q*ue* devian aver antiguame*n*te deve*n* ser del Rey, e puede las el dar aquie*n* se quisiere. E como quier que los Moros non tengan buena ley: pero mientra biviere*n* entre los Christianos en segurança dellos, no*n* les deven tomar, nin robar lo suyo por fuerça, e qualquier que contra esto fiziere mandamos que lo peche doblado todo lo que assi les tomare. (VII: 76^v)

Sarracenus, in Latin, means Moor, in Castilian, and this name is derived from Sarah, the free wife of Abraham, although the lineage of the Moors is not traced to her, but to Hagar, who was Abraham's servant. There are two kinds of Moors; some do not believe in either the New or Old Testament; the others accept the five books of Moses, but reject the Prophets and do not believe them. (V: 1438)

We decree that Moors shall live among Christians in the same way that we mentioned in the preceding Title [XXIV] that Jews shall do, by observing their own law and not insulting ours. Moors, however, shall not have mosques in Christian towns, or make their sacrifices publicly in the presence of men. The mosques which they formerly possessed shall belong to the king; and he can give them to whomsoever he wishes. Although the Moors do not acknowledge a good religion, so long as they live among Christians with their assurance of security, their property shall not be stolen from them or taken by force; and we order that whoever violates this law shall pay a sum equal to double the value of what he took. (V: 1438)

It follows then, that both Moors and Jews were treated with some measure of respect even though their belief and belief system[s] are, in the *Partidas*, clearly pronounced as contrary to the Christian Faith. The key here was that they were still allowed to live in Christian Spain amongst those who did not share in their personal convictions.[31] But there were severe punishments for those who prevented Muslims from converting to Christianity, while those Christians who converted to Islam are considered to be lunatics and condemned to death as heretics. It is interesting to note in this 25th title, that there is displayed considerable anxiety over the possibility

---

[31] In the final chapter concerning this project I tackle the position that Spain indeed was a space of some tolerance, and in fact allowed for such a myriad of cultural conflation to exist as an amalgam of Iberian representation and an order of sorts. My main support text shall be María Rosa Menocal's *The Ornament of the World: How Muslims, Jews, and Christians Created a Culture of Tolerance in Medieval Spain* (New York: Little, Brown and Company, 2002) alongside a close analysis of two Medieval Spanish poems—the *Auto* and the *Vida*—respectively.

of Christians converting to Judaism or Islam, which leads to a consideration of heresy in the 26th title which states in its introduction:

> Ereges son una manera de gente loca que se trabaja*n* de escatimar las palabras de nuestro Señor Jesu Christo, e les dan otro entendimiento contra a quel que los santos padres les diero*n*, e q*ue* la Eglesia de Roma cree: e manda guardar. (VII: 78[v])

> Heretics are a species of insane people who endeavor to pervert the sayings of Our Lord Jesus Christ, and impart to them a different construction from that which the Holy Fathers gave them and which the Church of Rome relieves, and orders to be observed. (V: 1443)

The "value" of the heretic according to Alfonso is that they are responsible for the tarnishing and disruption of a civil, peaceful society. Alfonso concludes in law I of this title, "Ca se trabajan siempre, de corromper las voluntades de los omes, e de los poner en error," ["Great injury results to a country from heretics of every description, for they constantly endeavor to corrupt the minds of men and cause them to err"] (VII: 78[v]; V: 1443). Alfonso continues to discuss the subject of the heretic via the following: who can accuse a heretic, the penalty of those who harbor heretics, while those who are heretics cannot hold any public office. In short, heretics were killed and stripped of their possessions and dignity. Anyone then contrary to the Faith, proved worthy of heretic[-al] status.

In analyzing the seventh *Partida* as well as the other sections in the *Partidas* already mentioned, we have witnessed the position of a Christian king, a learned man who desired to have a peaceful community patterned after Roman Civil Law, wherein justice was ultimate and an end in itself. The *Partidas* reveals not only a king and his court, but perhaps illuminates a thirteenth century society, and its attempts to convey the times via its literary output—where the subject of *magic*, either "black" or "white," could be privileged and communicated to a large readership. By aligning *magic* and its aberrant practices as against the Faith, but allowing non-Christian traditions to continue, one could argue that a "controlled," Alphonsan society, with competing traditions of Christian, Muslim and Jew existed; this type of quasi-tolerant community may have subsisted and most certainly may have flourished, especially in the communicative form of a literary exchange. By example, what follows is an examination of two poems, which concern the contribution of Spanish Literature and the subject of ("white") *magic*, or *miraculum* as well as the craft of Astrology, and the importance of the stars' determinant influence and prediction of the Divine royal order toward humankind. The texts we will be examining are: *Auto De Los Reyes*

Magos (*Auto*) and *La Vida De Santa María Egipcíaca* (*Vida*) — respectively.

CHAPTER THREE

Chapter 3 will develop an argument with regard to the perception and expression of *magic* as cultural awareness, albeit, as presented in the literary exchange of a given period; arguably, this awareness of *magic* begins from the classical period and extends into the modern one. For current purposes, however, I will confine my research to the examination of two significant poems from the Spanish Middle Ages, the *Auto de Los Reyes Magos* and the *Vida de Santa María Egipcíaca* (herein, *Auto* and *Vida*-respectively).

In examining the *Auto*, the role of magic and "religion," a term for my purpose interchangeable with "belief," is exemplified in the literary sense, which privileges the subject of Astrology, its practitioners, the "power" of Divine agency, and the dispensation of such power carried out in the explained phenomena of *miracula*. In parallel, the conflation of magic and religion, though present in the *Auto*, is best represented in the *Vida* amidst the episodes of its protagonist patterned after Saint Mary, an archetype of the Virgin Mary in name only. The poetic genre (*Auto* and *Vida*), I argue, showcases a didactic, moral discretion in which the subject of *miracula* is central to a Medieval Spanish understanding of the human realm; i.e. the [un]seen. As we have noted before, arguably "magic" in its bifurcation of terms—"black" and "white" is subjective, and while the former relies on demonic agency, it is the latter which concerns us here; i.e. "white" magic, as Jennifer M. Corry has asserted, is the explanation of phenomena via the Church. Magic, therefore, can be construed and couched within the sphere of power and agency given to the subject of *miracula*. Again, this point shall be central to our argument in the *Vida*. Magic is exemplified in this text as *miracula* and provides a window into the cultural milieu that existed during this time period within the early thirteenth century. Moreover, the country that allowed such literature to exist (namely Spain), perhaps, even represented a 'tolerant' land in which a wide array of competing beliefs and belief systems existed.

For this section of my project I will also look at the commentary afforded by two Spanish historians, Antonio Garrosa Resina and Julio Caro Baroja concerning the subject of magic in Spanish society. Moreover, the work by María Rosa Menocal, *The Ornament of the World: How Muslims, Jews, and Christians Created a Culture of Tolerance in Medieval Spain*, though controversial—will prove helpful when observing the Iberian

Penisula's affinity for a "mixed-bag" of cultural representation. In observing
Muslim, Jewish, and Christian traditions then, Spain provided a short-lived
example of tolerance for the remainder of the European continent. My hope
then is to entertain such inquiries as: *Why did Spain hold more tolerance
than the remainder of its European counterparts concerning the subject of
magic at this time?* and *If magic was indeed a viable subject of study, could
its practitioner offer moral direction, and could magic couched in literature
be didactic in its construction and provide a social analysis in its
application; moreover what were these wielders of the art called:
magicians, clergy, or both?* Such inquiries may indeed unlock or rather
uncover why today magic is still aligned with evil and hilarity instead of
perhaps examined as a viable belief and belief system that seeks to
understand the world; albeit, still an examination of the [un]known. It will
not, however, be part of my present scope to [re]examine or to [re]define a
specific Rhetoric of magic, or magic's distinct discourse system.[1]

3.1 Spanish Literature: A History of Ideas

We begin this chapter from the position of cultural identity in the
thirteenth century, wherein literature captured and articulated, albeit
imperfectly, the local "color" that was to be found within the Iberian
borders.[2] This is not an account of the political and other internal strife that

---

[1] In a future project, however, I do hope to extend my Iberian Peninsula thirteenth
century findings and track, via a trans-Atlantic migration, the position of "magic" in
America, and its dynamic influence upon the myriad of cultural artifacts found there:
media, literature, cinema, bumper stickers, et cetera. Essentially then, in such a
project I will dissertate that "magic" is imbued in much of the twenty-first century
acculturated *art* and literary forms, and that it survived many centuries of the
Church's disapproval and persecution only to spring up again in full force, as the
power and the authority of the Church gave way to secularizing forces.
[2] Julio Caro Baroja in his *Vidas Magicas e Inquisicion* (2 volumes, Madrid: Taurus
Ediciones, 1967) suggests:

En algún manual de Antropología acreditado se afirma que un método (harto
problemático, digo, por mi parte) que se ha solido usar para determinar el
"nivel" mental de una sociedad frente a otros es el de observar el grado de
efectividad que da la Magia en sus manifestaciones distintas. (1:23)

In a certain accredited manual of Anthropology (the reference is to A.L.
Kroeber, *Anthropology* [New York: Harcourt Brace, 1948], 48) it is asserted
that one method (albeit fully problematic, I suggest, for my part) that has
been solidly used to determine the mental "level" of one society with respect

marked Spain, but a look at what María Rosa Menocal, in part describes as, "the presence of Islam in Europe for the subsequent seven-hundred-odd-years, some three times the present duration of the American Republic," as an al-Andalus (the Arabic equivalent to Andalusia), and even more so, a Spain which harbored a mixture of cultures and "balanced" their existence accordingly (*The Ornament of the World*, 9).[3] Moreover, Menocal argues for a positive outcome that surrounded what I call cultural heterogeneity. She asserts, "This vision of a culture of tolerance recognized that incongruity in the shaping of individuals as well as their cultures was enriching and productive" (11). Surely, this was noted and supported by King Alfonso X in the kingdom of Castile-León and the remaining Andalusian South. Menocal, in utilizing F. Scott Fitzgerald's assertion that "the test of a first-rate intelligence is the ability to hold two opposed ideas in the mind at the same time," and in so doing suggests:

> In its moments of great achievement, medieval culture positively thrived on holding at least two, and often many more, contrary ideas at the same time. This was the chapter of Europe's culture when Jews, Christians, and Muslims lived side by side and, despite their intractable differences and enduring hostilities, nourished a complex culture of tolerance, and it is this difficult concept that my subtitle aims to convey. (11)

Menocal is referring to her subtitle, "How Muslims, Jews, and Christians Created a Culture of Tolerance in Medieval Spain." Indeed, the loaded term here, "create[ed]" is suggestive of a verb usage to perhaps inform, communicate, and articulate not in isolation per se, but toward the larger group (whoever they may be—Muslim, Jew, or Christian).[4] I attempt to

---

to others is to observe the degree of effect that magic gives in its distinct manifestations.
Baroja's point here is his hinting that the manual of *Anthropology* is in effect grading society: The more magic—the more "primitive"—the less magic, the more "civilized." Further, by observing the position of magic within a given culture, one can best observe that particular culture, thereby positing that magic is useful, more so as a barometer than a thermometer for the temperate pulse of the social strata.

[3] María Rosa Menocal's *The Ornament of the World: How Muslims, Jews, and Christians Created a Culture of Tolerance in Medieval Spain*, (New York: Little, Brown and Company, 2002), argues for an Iberian Peninsula, through its cultural heterogeneity, that privileged and provided, within a narrow window of time, balance; this equilibrium, rather than the term "stability" is what allowed for an existence of Muslim, Jews, and Christians alike.

[4] It is important to note that Menocal is referencing a triangulation of competing cultures: Muslim, Jewish, and Christian without conflation; where mixtures took

repeat her methodology, that is—"I have strung together a series of miniature portraits that range widely in time and place, and that are focused on cultural rather [than on] political events," though the literature to be considered is limited to two poems from the thirteenth century. The first from the early part of the century, the dramatic fragment in verse, *Auto de Los Reyes Magos* (herein, *Auto*) and the second, a poem in following the hagiographic structure that includes a sermon that corresponds with a Rhetorical narrative centered on Divine *beneficia* through the use of *miracula*, which collectively alongside the *Auto*, conveys themes of Christian responsibility, an ethic or code of moral behavior, and didactic reassurance in the penitent and obedient life through the literary device of poetry.

Arguably, the poem is also didactic and a mimetic representation of an Aristotelian past with regards to discerning one's world via the craft of Astrology, a divinatory "science." Literature, then, is the communicative medium which conveys at this time explanations of *miracula* and *beneficia*, which involves elements of "magic." I am here suggesting that *miracula* and magic are intertwined, thereby suggesting that examples of *miracula* are also examples of magic. Moreover, this Spanish poem from the thirteenth century is suggestive of a culture that not only understood its implications, but circulated and reaffirmed its position of belief and belief systems via such a *modus operandi*. What follows is an examination of Christian "magic," often referred to as "white" magic, in the short work known as the *Auto* followed by an analysis of Spanish tolerance.

3.2 Christian Magic: a Literary Exchange in the Explanation of Phenomena

The *Auto de Los Reyes Magos* (c.a. 1200, herein— *Auto*)[5] is a poem about the coming of the Son of God, the Christ, or if one prefers, the

---

place the Mozarabs, Conversos, and others of this heterogeneity became a quasi-homogeneity. Still, this is not her, nor this project's focus.

[5] The version of the thirteenth century anonymous poem that I utilized for this project is taken from the Biblioteca Nacionalde Madrid, Ms. Vit. 5-9 (*olim* Hh-105), fols 67-68[V] http://www.llc.manchester.ac.uk/subjects/splas//ug/documents/autrrmag_002.pdf, but utilized as an html: (http://64.233.167.104/search?q=cache:kzyrafdkjcij:www.art.man.ac.uk/spanish/ug/d ocuments/autrrmag_002.pdf+%22auto+de+los+reyes+magos%22&hl=en&ct=clnk& cd=12&gl=us), and the translation is based on a version by the American scholar Jim Marchand as revised by J. Lawrence; n.d. is given (retrieved on 9 June 2007).

Messiah. Essentially, the poem parallels the biblical story taken from the Gospel account of Matthew chapter 2, verses 1 through 12:

1. cum ergo natus esset Iesus in Bethleem Iudaeae in diebus Herodis regis ecce magi ab oriente venerunt Hierosolymam
2. dicentes ubi est qui natus est rex Iudaeorum vidimus enim stellam eius in oriente et venimus adorare eum
3. audiens autem Herodes rex turbatus est et omnis Hierosolyma cum illo
4. et congregans omnes principes sacerdotum et scribas populi sciscitabatur ab eis ubi Christus nasceretur
5. at illi dixerunt ei in Bethleem Iudaeae sic enim scriptum est per prophetam
6. et tu Bethleem terra Iuda nequaquam minima es in principibus Iuda ex te enim exiet dux qui reget populum meum Israhel
7. tunc Herodes clam vocatis magis diligenter didicit ab eis tempus stellae quae apparuit eis
8. et mittens illos in Bethleem dixit ite et interrogate diligenter de puero et cum inveneritis renuntiate mihi ut et ego veniens adorem eum
9. qui cum audissent regem abierunt et ecce stella quam viderant in oriente antecedebat eos usque dum veniens staret supra ubi erat puer
10. videntes autem stellam gavisi sunt gaudio magno valde
11. et intrantes domum invenerunt puerum cum Maria matre eius et procidentes adoraverunt eum et apertis thesauris suis obtulerunt ei munera aurum tus et murram
12. et responso accepto in somnis ne redirent ad Herodem per aliam viam reversi sunt in regionem suam[6]

2:1 When Jesus therefore was born in Bethlehem of Juda, in the days of king Herod, behold, there came wise men from the East to Jerusalem, *2:2* Saying: Where is he that is born king of the Jews? For we have seen his star in the East, and are come to adore him. *2:3* And king Herod hearing this, was troubled, and all Jerusalem with him. *2:4* And assembling together all the chief priests and the scribes of the people, he inquired of them where Christ should be born. *2:5* But they said to him: In Bethlehem of Juda. For so it is written by the prophet: *2:6* And thou Bethlehem the land of Juda art not the least among the princes of Juda: for out of thee shall come forth the captain that shall rule my people Israel. *2:7* Then Herod, privately calling the wise men learned diligently of them the time of the star which appeared to them; *2:8* And sending them into Bethlehem, said: Go and diligently inquire after the child, and when you have found him, bring me word again, that I also may come and adore him. *2:9* Who having heard the king, went their way; and behold the star which they had seen in the East, went before them, until it came and stood over where the child was. *2:10* And seeing the star they

---

[6] The Latin Vulgate is utilized here and the Douy-Rheims translation follows; the former can be found at: http://www.fourmilab.ch/etexts/www/vulgate/matthew.html; retrieved on 17 June 2007.

rejoiced with exceeding great joy. *2:11* And entering into the house, they found the child with Mary his mother, and falling down they adored him: and opening their treasures, they offered him gifts; gold, frankincense, and myrrh. *2:12* And having received an answer in sleep that they should not return to Herod, they went back another way into their country.[7]

The passage above is teeming with promising allusions concerning the subject of astrology as well as the practitioners who engaged in such an "art." The *Auto* seems to be incomplete, and though the poem is based on the previously quoted biblical passage, it suggests its own interpretation of the events that lead toward a "birthing" of the Christ child. Moreover, the poem in the context of thirteenth century Spanish culture allows for the Mozarabic residue to be found in Toledo during Muslim rule (c.a. 714-1085). That is, the text itself is written, though anonymously, in the Mozarabic dialect of Toledo. The first publication of the *Auto* was by Gottfried Baist, *Das altspanische Dreikönigsspiel: El Misterio de los reyes magos* (Erlangen, 1887), but it was Ramón Menéndez Pidal who titled the poem the *Auto de los Reyes Magos*. The poem directly concerns the validation of the Christ child as the new king in place of the present monarch, Herod the Great (ca. 73-4 BCE). Beneath such a simple plot rests the ultimate inquiry: *Of what purpose would a star serve,* and more still, *Of what value are those practitioners who are able to discern events via star gazing?*

If the heavens and its heavenly bodies offered signs and meaning to its onlookers, then practitioners of such an art must have provided some level of explanation as to what that particular meaning may have meant; and, repeated success at such divination may have marked them [the interpreters] as valuable assets in their starred *profession*. Historian Jack Lindsay in *Origins of Astrology* has suggested that Astronomy and Astrology went hand in hand and it was difficult to separate the two practices. Lindsay states:

> Astronomy could not be separated from Astrology, since practically all observers of the sky shared a concept of the divine nature of the bodies moving aloft, whether or not they agreed about the possibility of giving precise form to the influences emanating from above and of relating them to life on earth. (419)

---

[7] This version of the Bible is translated from the Latin in the Douay-Rheims version and can be found at: http://www.catholicfirst.com/searchengine.cfm?action=search; copyrighted 2000-2006; Catholic First; retrieved on 17 June 2007.

More recent scholarship by Sophie Page in *Astrology in Medieval Manuscripts* (herein, *Astrology*) suggests that "Writers employed the terms astronomy and astrology interchangeably, only using them in the modern sense when speaking of the two complementary aspects—theoretical and practical—of the same science of the stars" (*Astrology* 7). Wherein Astronomy participated in the observance of the stars that allowed humans to name and identify their universe—Astrology, "perceived symmetry between movements in the heavens and events on earth" (5). Once more, the former registers a nomenclature and identification of a given celestial phenomenon, while the latter ascribes a relevance of these phenomena to earthly events, to the lives of individuals, or to matters of communal concern such as crops going bad because of heavenly *dis*order[s]. Such distinctions or conflations will not necessarily need disentanglement here, but what is of interest is that such subjects of study were being taught at the University during the thirteenth century as part of the *trivium* and *quadrivium*; moreover, both had their overlapping presence in the first of the two poems we will examine in this third chapter.

The *Auto* begins with an open dialogue between the three *Reys* as they each give turn to understanding and interpreting the position of a "new" star alongside the "birth" of the "new" king in Christ.[8] The first Rey opens with:

Dios criador, quál maraviella.
no sé cual es aquella strella;
agora primas la é veída,
poco tiempo ha que es nacida.

---

[8] Antonio Garrosa Resina from his *Magia y Superstición: en la Literatura Castellana Medieval* comments:

Los detalles fantásticos de este fragmentario texto dramático […] que sólo conocemos ciento cuarenta y siete versos, están todos relacionados con el oficio de astrólogo de los tres Magos protagonistas y con su facultad de observar las estrellas e interpretar las señales advertidas en ellas. (52)

The fantastic details of this fragmentary dramatic text […] of which we only know one hundred forty seven verses, are all interconnected with the craft of Astrology of the three wise men [literal-magicians] as protagonists and with their ability to observe the stars and interpret the signs as conveyed by them.

Garossa Resina is aware that this poem is concerned with not just a mere, religious audience, but perhaps one in which the position of Astrology could not be seen as foreign nor completely a conflation from or against a religious ideal-to interpret, via signs, one's world view; again, the explanation of phenomena, the birth of God in Christ, was both. Remember that Isidore of Seville has asserted that Astrology was a viable science before the gospel narratives—it is his claim that it subsequently ceased to be valid that is being challenged in a text such as this.

¿Nacido es el Criador
que es de la' gentes señor? (lines 1-6)[9]

God the Creator, what a marvel.
I do not know this star;
this is the first time I have seen it,
it was born only a little time ago.
Has the Creator been born, he who is Lord of nations?

These first six lines set the stage and tone for the remainder of the poem. By opening with "quál maraviella," ["what a marvel"] (line 1) we note that both *mirabilia* and *miraculum* give shape to such a description of wonder, namely that the Creator himself is the subject of such an opening! This is no benediction, for what follows is the first Rey's anxiety of the unknown, or in this sense the unrecognized. He admits that it is indeed a star, but one that eludes his skill set. Moreover, this is confirmed by his question, "¿Nacido es el Criador / que es de la' gentes señor?," ["Has the Creator been born, / he who is Lord of nations?"] (lines 5-6). What is of great interest here is the alignment of the birth of a star alongside the birth of a Savior. In other words, this first Rey recognizes that perhaps both births are intertwined and give rise to the astrological implications that each person has a star under the zodiac registry (recall, this has been looked at already elsewhere in Chapter 2). In line with this questioning the first Rey continues to address his anxiety at the mere thought of a new star and the new Christ by the use of a scientific method or reasoning of sorts. Rey number one asserts, "Otra noche me lo cataré, / si es vertad bien lo sabré." ["I shall observe it another night, / if it's true I shall know for sure."] (lines 9-10). Finally, after further enquiry he decides to believe that this new star is a sign that:

Aquesto es, y non es ál:
nacido es Dios, por ver, de fembra
en aquest mes de deciembre.
Allá iré, ó que fuere, aorarlo é,
por Dios de todos lo terné. (lines 14-18)

It's this, and nothing else:
God is born, verily, of a woman
in this month of December.
I'll go wherever he is, and worship him,
I'll hold him to be God of all men.

---

[9] The play is divided by some scholars into five scenes: Scene I, lines 1-51; Scene II, lines 52-73; Scene III, lines 76-114; Scene IV, lines 115-31; Scene V, lines 137-57. The attribution of speakers to text is editorial as speakers are not identified in the MS.

Rey number one finalizes his assertion in the oscillating tone of a confessional and a declaration, and prepares the way for another layering of investigation with reference to this event. The poem shifts to Rey number two and his response concerning the position and meaning of the particular star. Seemingly, Rey number two is lost though he adds that these events could be judged in a more secular setting, to be precise of things pertaining to the earth and the ordering of an operation pertinent to an earthly child birth. The second Rey states:

> Esta strella non sé dónd viene,
> quién la trae o quién la tiene.
> ¿Por qué es aquesta señal?
> En m[i]os días non vi atal.
> Certas nacido es en tierra
> aquel qui en pace y en guerra
> señor ha a seer da oriente
> de todos hata en occidente. (lines 19-26)

> I don't know where this star comes,
> who brings it or who holds it.
> What does this sign mean?
> In all my days I never saw such a thing.
> Surely he is born on earth
> who, in peace and war,
> will be lord of all men
> from the east to the far west.

He further suggests that he is to keep a "watch" on the star for an additional three nights so that he may gather a bit more information and make an educated guess as it were.[10] Rey number two, though unsure of the star's significance, is privileged by the poet to still go out toward the East and, in following the star, locate and worship the Christ child. He states:

---

[10] *La Méthode Scientifique*, or the Scientific Method, a prescriptive attempt at producing reproducible results after an elaborate array of investigative measures regarding science and/or observation of one's world is clearly at use here. The steps involved are as follows; first, one is to identify and define the problem; second, then to make observations; third, look for regularities; fourth, to wonder why such regularities exist; fifth, to propose a hypothesis, or educated and best-informed guess; sixth, to test one's hypothesis via an experiment; lastly, to obtain reproducible results. The Magi are indeed fulfilling some, if not all, of these prescriptive measures to obtain their answer[s].

Non sé si algo he veído.
Iré, lo aoraré,
Y pregaré y rogaré. (lines 31-3)

I don't know if I've seen something
I'll go and adore him,
and I'll pray and beseech.

This stubborn belief without a sure footing could be considered a *faith* as conflated by a pagan astrologer. This is where magic and faith inter-connect as well as magic and science. However, we are unsure of the position that an astrologer warrants in the poem, and in fact the reader does not receive this until the third Rey is introduced. As he has been observing alongside the other two Reys, the third Rey states, "Val Criador," ["God help me"] (line 33a) and pragmatically asserts:

Tal estrella non es in cielo,
desto só yo bono strellero;
que uno omne es nacido de carne
que es señor de todo el mundo
así cumo el cielo es redondo. (lines 36-41)

Nacido es el Criador,
de todas las gentes mayor;
bien lo [v]eo que es verdad.
Iré allá, par caridad. (lines 48-51)

There is no such star in the sky,
I am a good enough astrologer for this;
I see it well, without foolery,
that a man is born of flesh
who is lord of all the world
as far as the sky around.

The Creator is born,
the elder of all the nations;
I can see very well that it's true.
I shall go there, by God's love.

It takes then, the third Rey to admit that he is a "good enough astrologer" for making a judgment on this particular star that rests in the East. And when asked again by Rey number one, "Dios vos salve, señor, / ¿sodes vós strellero? ["God save you, sir; are you an astrologer?"] (lines 52-4), the response is assertive and fittingly practical as Rey number three states:

[Nacida] es una strella.
Nacido es el Criador
que da las gentes es señor.
Iré, lo aoraré. (lines 57-60)

A star is born.
Born is the Creator
who is Lord of the nations.
I shall go and adore him.

With such resolve from Rey number three the other two Reys, though still unconvinced, desire to follow the star in hopes to find the Creator. The poem then shifts from validation of the star's significance back to placing the onus on the Christ child. In determining whether the child is of the secular, earthly realm or of the heavenly, divine circle, Rey number three suggests an experiment is in order. He states:

¿Queredes biene saber cúmo lo sabremos?
Oro, mirra y encenso a él ofreçremos:
si fuere rei de tierra, el oro querrá;
si fuere omne mortal, la mirra tomará;
si rei celestial, estos dos dexará,
tomará el encenso quel' perteneçra. (lines 69-74)

Do you want to know how we will know?
We shall offer him gold, myrrh, and incense:
if he is an earthly king he will take the gold,
if he is a mortal man he will take myrrh,
if a celestial king he will leave these two
and take the incense, which will be his.

There is a moral, as well as, a didactic attempt to suggest the character of a child, regardless of age, to *know* a "good" or a "bad" from each other, and in making such choices, the "truth" not only ensue, but should materialize. Still, the three Reys make their decision and after much observation and investigation, step out [in "faith"] toward their objective, which is simply to recognize and worship the child who is born under this particular star. The scene shifts rather quickly, and though demarcated by such arbitrary markings as the line numbers imposed upon by its editors, the poem seems disjointed. Caspar, one of the Reys on the pilgrimage to locate the Christ child comes across the current king, Herod the Great. As Caspar tells the king of his journey we learn the other names of the Reyes collectively known now as: Caspar, Melchior, and Balthazar. Further, when Herod is informed by Caspar of the new king he is not pleased and asks an array of

questions that attempt to arrive at an understanding of how such things can
be. Herod, feverishly asks, "¿Y cúmo lo abedes? / ¿Ya provado lo avedes?"
["And how do you know? / Have you proof of it already?"] (lines 96-7).
Clearly, the Rhetoric here is one of science and investigative science at that.
In lines 98 through 109 we are told by one of the Reyes (the poem does not
inform the reader as to who it is that spoke, whether it was Rey one, two, or
three) that their "proof" consists in their diligent observations for a span of
about thirteen days, and that their interpretation of the star as a sign of such a
"birth," though of great *mirabilia*, is sound and "true." Initially, king
Herod's reply seems genuinely commensurate with the other Reyes' desire
to locate and worship the Christ child. This however is not to be the case as
the poet privileges a dialogue concerning the true nature of the "usurped"
king's mind. The poet allows us inside the mind of Herod and presents a
rather angry monarch as he states:

> ¿Quién vio nuncas tal mal
> sobre rei otro tal?
> Aún non so yo muerto,
> ni so la terra puesto!
> rei otro sobre mí?
> Nuncas atal non vi!
> El sieglo va a çaga,
> ya non sé qué me faga;
> por vertud no lo creo
> ata que yo lo veo. (lines 115-24)

> Who ever saw such evil,
> one king over another!
> I am not yet dead
> or buried in the earth:
> another king over me?
> I never saw such a thing!
> The world is upside down,[11]
> I no longer know what to do;
> I won't believe it's true
> until I see him.

---

[11] The inversion of ideas is commensurate here with Herod's position that, "El sieglo
va a çaga, / ya non sé qué me faga;" ["The world is upside down, / I no longer know
what to do"], and as such suggests that at the limits of human reason and
understanding what is necessary is something greater, something more, something
that understands and reveals such a phenomena; this event of another king for Herod
is a simple rival until he realizes, or attempts to realize the importance of the
announcement and the star that signifies its "proof."

Herod, the empiricist reflects the earlier anxieties that each Rey respectively and collectively conveyed; the didactic message here, however, is that there is a difference between doubting and not responding and doubting, but trusting in the [un]seen for clarification on the matter. Herod is working under a different motivation for gaining the whereabouts of this young king. In his distress Herod desires answers for himself and turns to the doctors of the law[s] and magicians and astrologers who, in utilizing the tangible, reflected here as the "literature," should be learnèd enough to provide the king with an understanding. One can imagine Herod with hands held high and a threatening glare shouting:

> Venga mi maiordo[mo]
> qui mios averes toma.
> Idme por mios abades
> y por mis podestades
> y por mios scrivanos
> y por mios gramatgos
> y por mios strellros
> y por mios retoricos:
> dezirm' han la vertad
> si yace in escripto
> o si lo saben ellos
> o si lo han sabido. (lines 125-36)

> Summon my chamberlain
> who collects my Money.
> Go fetch my abbots
> and my potentates
> and my scribes
> and my magicians
> and my astrologers
> and my orators:
> they will tell me the truth
> if it is written down,
> or if they know it
> or if they have heard it.

Herod's reliance on what I call, his "informed armada," positions the magician and the astrologer as well as the abbots and scribes in a tangential, though vertical hierarchy in which information is the "name of the game." Why? Herod is in search of "la vertad," or the "truth" concerning the Christ, therefore, positioning the Christ child as such an amalgam of inquiry, that it will take all of Herod's informed armada to elucidate this rather dark and cloudy event. Upon their arrival, Herod has but one question at the top of his list—"¿Y traedes vostros escriptos?" ["And have you brought your books?"] (line 138). In the king privileging the position of learning via books, it is clear that this branch of epistemology can disentangle the events of the world, even events that include the birth of God in the similitude of humankind under a specific, though "unrecognizable" star. As Herod engages with his subjects to verify the Christ child, we note yet another shift from the poet as he privileges the uselessness of the Rabí. Perhaps, in showcasing their limited knowledge it could conceivably be an attack on the Jewish tradition as a whole, but there is not enough evidence to warrant this, and because of the unfinished poem, closure on the matter is not to be expected. One final caveat though does allow for a possible, hopeful reinstated Jewish position, and it stems from the Rabí number two as he states:

Hamihalá,[12] cumo eres enartado!
¿Por qué eres rabí clamado?
¿Non entiendes las profecías,
las que nos dixo Jeremías?
Par mi lei, nós somos errados.
¿Por qué non somos acordados,
Por qué non dezimos vertad? (lines 149-54)

Al-amdu li-llāh, how crafty you are
Why are you called rabbi?
Do you not understand the prophecies
that Jeremiah told us?
By my Law, we have gone astray.
Why haven't we come to our senses
why don't we tell the truth?

The "truth" is what Herod is seeking and in looking to obtain even some modicum of its substance in the written text[s] is told by one of his trusted advisers that "truth" is not to be found. Where then shall truth be found? The answer lies within the mouth of the first Rabí, as he suggests, "¡Yo non la se, par caridad!" ["I don't know the truth, for charity's sake!"] (line 155). In looking for truth then, like Herod and the Magi respectively, one notices that the search is complemented via the source or motive for the search; for the Magi, via the use of astrology and "faith" in the form of the stubborn resolve

---

[12] "Hamihalá" put in the mouth of the second rabbi is a form of the Qū'ranic phrase: "Al-hamda li-llāh" ("All praise belongs to allah"); an incongruence utterance in the mouth of a Jewish holy man, but a good example of the syncretic Mozarabic dialect of the Spanish of Toledo at the time.

in which their pilgrimage was begun; contrastingly, for Herod, his motive for the extinction of a rival amidst the useless informants that comprised the learnèd without "faith," their results, as we have seen, were null and void.

The *Auto* presents a poem that leaves much to be desired and, though itself a short work of approximately 150 lines, it provides a wealth of allusions to the subject of belief and *miracula* as well as magic couched in Astrology and divination. Herod's fear[s] and apprehension is not without good foundation. As king his rule must be absolute, and a new upstart without his informant's knowing and telling him about it prove problematic. Perhaps, the author was trying to make light of the matter of competitive rule, where the disputing regimes involve a Divine child, or that which resides in the heavens and the secular rule, or that which pertained to matters on Earth.[13]

Arguably, one could claim that where Astrology and Astronomy are concerned—being in the know is of greater interest than established, uninformed, common, earthly and secular rule where information is impoverished. The advantage surely goes to that practice or "art," which suggests answers to phenomena where earthly knowledge is not only lacking, but severely derisory. Hence, as we began this analysis Herod is still poised to learn of this new event, but attempts to hear it from his earthly pawns. The *Auto de los Reyes Magos* further provides perhaps a rather biased and didactic message—one in which Jennifer M. Corry asserts:

> Just as Christianity sought to prevail over older traditions, the Three Kings must prevail in this Christian story. The contrast that the Kings present to the court rabbis demonstrates the author's vision of the new replacing the old; Christianity will reign superior over all prior religions and beliefs. The Magi's astrology is acceptable because it announces the divine birth. A medieval audience could intuit that God has allowed foresight of this event. (*Perceptions* 130)

Of interest here is how Corry interpolates the position of religion (Church) as a dominant force, so much so that it too gets to wield magic for its own purpose[s]. This thesis follows the common thread throughout this project, namely the ambiguities of magic and its affectations, and provides perhaps beginning examinations that in order to better understand religion and science, one must enter through the gate of "magic". Jennifer M. Corry

---

[13] Suggestive of the poet's competing power struggles regarding complete governance as a poetic device aligns itself rather coincidentally with arguably, a Spain that saw plenty of unrest and many warring factions competing for the Iberian affection of all. Still, nothing can be guaranteed that this is what the poet had in mind, though it provides some element of the medieval mind.

examines various centuries regarding Spanish Literature, and her close
analysis through a feminist critique, suggests that the role of the goddess has
been replaced by the patriarchic Church. For this project, I have utilized her
analysis of the thirteenth century as it pertained to magic and *miraculum* in
the literary genre. Further, Corry suggests: "The literature of the thirteenth
century presents a variety of magical practitioners and miracle workers,
which reflects the varied ideas about magic that were typical of the time"
(*Perceptions* 152). Her thinking is not alone and in fact echoes that of Julio
Caro Baroja as he asserts in his *Vidas Magicas Inquisicion* (herein, *Vidas
Magicas*):

> De acuerdo con ella, no hay modo de hacer una distinción tajante entre
> Magia y Religión, en el sentido en que la hicieron autores tan divergentes
> como Frazer, de un lado, y Graebner o el padre Schmidt, de otro, y después
> de estos teóricos, otros antropólogos de campo, para aplicarla de modo
> general y sistemático a sociedades muy distintas. (27)

> Pues bien, según es sabido, tres famosos antropólogos construyeron tres
> teorías de la Magia (que se han considerado encontradas), exagerando bien
> al lado intelectual (Magia como seudo ciencia), bien el lado inmoral (Magia
> como actividad antisocial), bien el lado emocional (Magia como actividad
> pasional)…

> Esto no quiere decir […] que las "dicotomías" Magia-Religión y Magia-
> Ciencia sean inútiles por completo, como herramientos de averiguación.
> Pueden ser erróneas si se toman en un sentido absoluto, pero no si se
> consideraran parcialmente… (27-28)

> In accordance with it [magic], there is no method to make a sharp distinction
> between Magic and Religion, in the sense that such divergent authors have
> done like Frazer,[14] on one side, and Graebner[15] or Father Schmidt,[16] on
> another, and after these theorists, other anthropologists of this camp, to apply
> in general and systematic fashion to distinct societies.

> Well and good, it is known, three famous anthropologists constructed three
> theories of Magic (that have been considered as conflicting), exaggerating

---

[14] Sir James Frazer (1854-1941), one of the most prominent members of the
Cambridge School of Anthropolgy which saw human behavior in terms of ritual.
Most famous for his *The Golden Bough: A Study in Magic and Religion*, 3rd ed., 12
vols. (New York: Macmillan, 1935).
[15] Fritz Graebner (1887-1934). Ethnologist best known for his *Das Weltbild der
Primitiven* (Munich: Ernst Reinchardt, 1924).
[16] William Scmidt (1868-1954). Theologian and Ethnographer; his primary work is
Der Ursprung des Gottesidee, 12 vols. (Münster: Aschendorf, 1912-1955).

either the intellectual side (Magic as pseudo-science), well the immoral side (Magic as anti-social activity), as the emotional side (Magic as a passionate activity).

This does not mean to suggest […] that the "dichotomies" Magic-Religion and Magic-Science are completely useless, like tools of exploration. These can be erroneous if they are taken in the absolute sense, but not if they are considered partially and in context.

It seems then where contrariety of subjects exist that contrariety of ideas should follow, but such was not the case in Spain. As we have noted, the *Auto* reflected a mixture of ideas. Though in a creative genre, it still presents the distilled product of a tolerant community aware of the varied ideas presented; Religion and Pseudo-Science; Belief and Observation; and even Religion and Magic as well as Science [Astrology] and Magic. According to María Rosa Menocal in her seminal work *The Ornament of the World* she asserts:

> The very heart of culture as a series of contraries lay in al-Andalus, which requires us to reconfigure the map of Europe and put the Mediterranean at the center, and begin telling at least this part of our story [of tolerance in Spain] from an Andalusian perspective. It was there that profoundly Arabized Jews rediscovered and reinvented Hebrew; there that Christians embraced nearly every aspect of Arabic style—from the intellectual style of philosophy to the architectural styles of mosques […] This vision of a culture of tolerance recognized the incongruity in the shaping of individuals as well as their cultures was enriching and productive. (11)

It was because of such Islamic transformation and its desire to impart such great wisdom to an Iberian people that the mixed cultures, though true to its own, respective traditions, could not help but receive the infectious and overlapping traditions of others. Menocal asserts that it was the Arab-Islamic civilization which "out of their acquisitive confrontation with a universe of languages, cultures, and people, the Umayyads, who had come pristine out of the Arabian desert, defined their version of Islam as one that loved its dialogues with other traditions" (21). The appreciation and fondness for other traditions is what, in part, allowed for a quasi-tolerant Iberian Peninsula. Further, as the expectation of political unification under the administration of Alfonso IX, Ferdinand III, and James I, and as we have already discussed elsewhere, Alfonso X suggests, a social tolerance, though short-lived was underway. Where compromise of traditions existed, one could argue that the price for a "tolerant" society was a loss of that society's identity; i.e. where community benefited, a specific group, in time, could arguably lose its independent cultural identity due to the overlapping influences of their respective neighbors.

Menocal, in addressing the significant attainment regarding Islamic appeal to other socio-cultural noramtives suggests that "this was a remarkable achievement, so remarkable in fact that some later Muslim historians accused the Umayyads of being lesser Muslims for it" (24). Conversely, the position of the Mozarabs and Spanish Conversos also faced similar judgment, and "Christian" Alfonso's *Partidas*, though suggesting a peaceful union toward other races: Muslim and Jews—respectively outlined how they are to live and behave in the midst of a towering Church-dominated society. Further, the Iberian Mudejars, Muslims who lived in Christian cities, also contributed to such a mixture within an already mélange and "balanced" society.

3.3 Magic, Miracula & Mimesis

On examination the didactic and heavily sermonized poem, *Vida de Santa María Egipcíaca* (herein, *Vida*), reveals the dispensation of Divine grace and makes a didactic appeal to living an obedient life. We shall begin with a brief synopsis of the poem, and then proceed to a more careful analysis taken with *miraculum*, the Church's central explanation of magic via phenomena, in tow, and privileging specific occurrences of this particular phenomenon through the life of the author's protagonist, Santa María de Egipcíaca, ["Saint Mary of Egypt"]. According to M. Sciavonne de Cruz-Saenz in *The Life of Saint Mary of Egypt*, "The earliest known version of the legend of Saint Mary of Egypt is in Greek and has been attributed to Sophronius, Patriarch of Jerusalem (d. 639), and that furthermore, "the story [itself] dates from the second half of the fifth century" (11). From this Sophronian legend there are three Latin versions of the poem, most commonly identified by the sigla P, C, and A. For our purposes we are interested in the poetic *vita* of Saint Mary. Cruz-Saenz suggests that the poem "exists in whole or in part in one Old Spanish and eight Old French manuscripts ranging from the first years of the thirteenth century to the fourteenth century; again, we will analyze the Old Spanish late thirteenth to early fourteenth century version. This particular MS is currently preserved in the Biblioteca del Escorial.[17] The *Vida* can be sectioned into four distinct

---

[17] Cruz-Saenz asserts that this MS K:
   Is well-known, and its history has been at least partially documented. It
   probably belonged to the library of Jerónimo Zurita, whose manuscripts were
   deposited in the monastery of Aula Dei in Zaragoza in 1571. The manuscript

sections; first, lines 1-205 discuss the grace and mercy of God, Mary's disillusionment with her life in her parental home, and her lascivious and lustful life there, as well as her departure to Alexandria at the age of twelve; second, lines 206-453 discuss Mary's journeying with pilgrims to Jerusalem to which she offers her body as payment of the trip and later the miraculous impediment to her entering the Church based on Mary's sins of lust and prostitution; third, lines 454-1218 present a transformed Mary, upon being unable to enter the Temple, Mary fixes on the image of the Virgin Mary— repents, enters the Church, buys three loaves of bread, then crosses the Jordan to spend forty years in the desert; later, she is encountered by Zozimás of the monastery of St. John, whom she knows all about thanks to a vision of the Virgin; in their meeting each of them asks for the other's mutual blessing, which takes place; lastly, in lines 1219-1452, Mary separates from Zozimás to continue her penance as he returns to the Jordan, Mary dies and Zozimás is entrusted with her interment through the assistance of a lion, and Zozimás in some final exhortations admonishes the Church in a reflection of the penitent life of now Saint Mary.

The poet of the *Vida* introduces María as a young woman who is far too independent:

De pequenya fue bautizada,
malamientre fue ensenyada.
Mientre que fue en mancebía,
dexó bondat e priso follía:
tanto fue plena de luxuria
que non entendie otra curia. (lines 83-88)

As a child she was baptized,
badly she was educated,
while she was in childhood,
she repudiated the shame and took up a life of sin:
so much was she full of lechery
that she was not interested in any other preoccupation.

---

later turned up in the library of the Conde Duque de Olivares, where it was given the number still legible today, "Caj. 2, num. 17". (27)
The version of the *Vida* that I will be utilizing for this project is the one by Manuel Alvar, *Vida de Santa María Egipciaca*, 2 vols. (Madrid: C.S.I.C., 1970-73). It should be noted that Rodríguez de Castro "first referred to the manuscript as being of the thirteenth century" (27) as referenced by Cruz-Saenz. Regardless, we will proceed with an examination of a poem that more than likely began in the Old Spanish from the Old French in the late thirteenth to early fourteenth century.

Here we find a Mary that is anything but saintly as she is fully immersed in the ways of excess, and in context with her lust and immoral behavior, one need not go too far as to suggest via the poet, "que non entendie otra curie," ["that she was not interested in any other *pre*occupation"] (line 88). Her business of course involved her body as currency and conduit for pleasure; such physical hedonism proved commensurate with a reprobate mind and the poet in making Mary an example promotes a most worthy sinner. He continues to describe Mary as being: "tanto bella e genta, / mucho fiaba en su juventa;" ["so beautiful and gracious / she trusted much in her youth"] (89-90) to the distress of her parents whose response is appropriate to her shocking behavior: "Sus parientes, cuand' la veién, / por poco que se non murién," ["Her parents, when they saw her, / almost perished at her sight"] (101-02). In lines 135 through 204 the reader witnesses a Mary who departs to Alexandria for a good time, for the "excitement" of city life; i.e. the proverbial lights, and stars, imbued with dance, pomp and music. What is more, her departure, like a thief, is reminiscent of Jesus' claims that his return would be in a similar manner as a thief.[18] The poet has a clear understanding of the Gospel narrative[s] and appears well-versed concerning the didactic and moral codes as well as the stringent methodology or the conviction utilized to anchor *ecclesia* sanction. The poet states: "Sola salló como ladrón, / que non demandó companyón," ["Alone she departed like a thief, / who did not desire any [travel] companion"] (lines 139-40). Her life in Alexandria was one filled with vice and sexual immorality and she entertained a steady flow of men who, as the text suggests: "Todos la hi van corteyar / por el su cuerpo alabar," ["All (the men) came to court her / in order to praise her body"] (159-61); moreover, Mary continues in Alexandria at such a pace that she lived carousingly and at one point the poet reiterates: "En Alexandria era María: / Asi s' mantenié noche e día; / en Alesandria era venida, / ahí mantenié aquesta vida," ["In Alexandria was Mary: / There she supported herself night and day [via lust]; / in Alexandria she had arrived, / and there she lives this kind of life"] (lines 195-98). Lines 205 through 260 privileges a snapshot of Mary's outward appearance and beauty, that commodity by which she continued to live out her wildest sexual fancies. The poet states:

---

[18] It is not a far stretch to align many of the cursory descriptions which pertain to Mary on the superficial *nivel*, but baring further investigation, the position of thief align with Jesus' warning for his followers and Christians, or "little Christs," to be alert and ready for the unannounced return of the Son; the warning can be found in the Gospel According to Matthew 24:38-44.

De la beltat de su figura,
como dize la escriptura,
ante que siga adelante,
direvos de su semblante:
de aquel tiempo que fue ella,
depués no nasció tan bella;
nin reina nin condessa
non viestes otra tal como essa.
Abié redondas las orejas,
blanquas como leche d'ovejas;
ojos negros, e sobreçejas;
abla fruente, fasta la çernejes
La faz tenié colorada,
como la rosa cuando es granada;
boqua chica e por mesura
muy fermosa la catadura.
Su cuello e su petrina
tal como la flor dell espina.
De sus tetiellas bien es sana
tales som como maçana. (lines 205-24)

Of the beauty of her figure [appearance],
as the text says,
before one goes forward,
we will speak of her [Mary's] countenance:
from that time that she lived,
was never afterward any born so beautiful;
neither queen nor countess
nor saw you anyone like her.
She had round ears,
white like ewe's milk;
black eyes, and eyebrows;
white forehead, almost white her hair.
Her face was red,
like the rose when it blooms;
a small mouth and for good measure
very noble her gaze.
Her neck and her breast
[were] just [white] as the hawthorne flower.
Concerning her very healthy breasts,
each was like an apple.

This gives an account of Mary's physical beauty, and as the poem has depicted, this is a Mary who is enjoying her youthful good looks no matter what the cost. When Mary encounters a group of pilgrims en route to Jerusalem she too wants to come along, although since she has neither gold nor silver for the journey, she will serve the pilgrims on the voyage with her body. When she arrives at Jerusalem she joins the procession on the feast of the Assumption.[19] However, Maria finds that her entry into the Church is encumbered by some unknown or rather unseen force. The poet states:

El día vino de la Ascensión,
allí fue grant proçessión
de los pelegrinos de ultramar,
que van al templo a Dios rogar.
Los buenos omnes e los romeros
al templo van a rogar a Deus.
Non se perçibio María,
metiósse entr'ellos en companyía
Metiósse entr'ellos en proçessión,
mas non por buena entençión.
Los peregrinos, cuando la veyén,
su corazón non gelo sabién.
Que si ellos sopiessen qui es Maria
no aurién con ella fecho companyía.
A las puertas vinién a los grados
a el templo son entrados.
Dentro entró la companyía,
mas non y entro María.
En la grant priessa dentro se metié,
mas nulla re no le valié.
Que assí le era assemejant
que veyé huna gente muy grant
en semejança de caualleros,
mas semejábanle muy fieros.
Cada uno tenié la su espada,
menazábanla a la entrada.
Cuando querié adentro entrar,
ariedro la fazién tornar.
Cuando vio que non podié aber la entrada,
atrá faze la su tornada. (lines 424-53)

The day of Ascension arrived,
there was a great procession
of the pilgrims from overseas,
who go to the Temple[20] to pray to God.

---

[19] This feast is celebrated on August 15.
[20] This is presumably a reference to the large Church on the Temple Mount dedicated to the Virgin Mary built during the reign of the Emperor Justinian (c. 527-65). Before it was destroyed it was a popular destination for pilgrims.

The good people and the pilgrims
go to the Temple to pray to God.
Mary was unaware,
went with the others in the company,
went with the others in the procession,
but not out of good intentions.[21]
The pilgrims when they saw her,
they did not know her intention.
Had they known that it was that Mary
they would not have had her in their company.
Gradually they approached the doors
and within the Temple they enter.
The company entered into it [the Temple],
but Mary was unable to enter there.
That great crowd which entered there
no good did it do her.
For thus was appearing to her
that she saw a great crowd of people,
in likeness, of knights [warriors],
but looking very fierce.
Each one carried a sword,
they threatened her at the [Temple] entrance.
When she desired to enter inside,
they made her turn back.
When she knew she was not able to make an entrance,
She made a retreat from there.

The message here is a clear one—those who engage in such sins as what
Mary had immersed herself into—are not welcomed into the presence of
God's holy sanctuary, especially one dedicated to the Virgin Mary as this
one appears to be. The text makes it clear that Mary lacked the spiritual
requirements that would grant her access into such a space for worship and
prayer and "beseechment" of God. Again, Mary does not belong.

The poet chooses this particular episode in the poem to suggest a "reality
check" within Mary and produces her first, true attempt at repentance. In her
contrition, Mary offers up a prayer and in receiving some Divine guidance
utters in despair, "Dios dame la muerte," ["God grant me death"] (line 473).
Concerning such a death, Mary may have requested a physical absolvement
from her present sinful life, however, there is penance to be served and

---

[21] The French text says, however: "mais quant les aperćut Marie / mist sois en cele
compaignie, / mist soi en le procession, / nient par bone entencion" (But when Mary
saw them / she placed herself in the company, / she placed herself in the procession, /
but not for good intention) (lines 367-70; Alvar 121).

casualty will arrive, but it will first present itself as a physical decay and decline of all the comforts associated with a fit body. Further, Mary sees a statue of the Virgin to which she immediately addresses her prayers for forgiveness (483-86, 488-607). Making her plea for forgiveness, she submits to the divine will: "alço sus manos amas, / e ayuntó amas sus palmas," ["she raised both her hands, / raised them open-palmed (toward Heaven)] (lines 612-13). For her humility, Mary is then rewarded by being able to enter the Temple and to hear the teachings and engage in prayers with the other Temple worshippers. It is then that she hears that:

> Una boz oyó veramente,
> que le dixo paladinamente:
> —"Ve a la ribera de flum Jordán,
> al monasterio de sant Johan.
> Una melezina prenderás,
> de todos tus pecados sanarás:
> Corpus Cristo te darán
> e flum Jordán te passarán;
> Depués entrarás en hun yermo,
> morarás hi un grant tiempo.
> En el yermo estarás;
> fasta que bivas, hi despendrás."
> Cuando ella oyó esta santa boz,
> en la su fruente fizo la cruz. (632-45)

> Clearly she heard a voice,
> which said to her openly:
> —"Go to the bank of the river Jordan,
> to the Monastery of St. John.
> A cure you will take,
> which will wipe away all your sins:
> The Eucharist they will give to you
> and over the river Jordan will you go;
> then you will enter a barren place,
> and you will live there a long time.
> In the barren [desert] will you reside;
> while you live, you will atone for them [your past sins]."
> When Mary heard this saintly voice,
> she made the sign of the cross in front of herself.

In search of the monastery Mary then begins her arduous journey, and on the way out of the city she encounters a pilgrim who is kind enough to give her three small coins with which she is able to buy three loaves of bread. It is in the desert that she encounters the devil and truly begins her penance (lines 676-83). In these lines the poet states:

María de andar non fina,
mas non olvida a la reïna,
la que metiera por fiador
ante la imagen de su senyor,
que por su mercé non la dexasse,
e del diablo la anparasse.
En ella mete la su creyença;
agora comienza su penitençia. (676-83)

Mary was not done traveling,
moreover, she did not forget the Queen,[22]
she whom w\she had taken as protector
before the image of the Lord [in the temple],
and through her mercy She did not forsake her,
and protected her from the devil.
In Her did she place her faith;
and now begins her penitence

The harsh treatment of the desert and the lack of sustainable particulars, such as food (beyond the three loaves of bread and water from the riverbed) and clothing, take their toll and her once external beauty, which once amassed compliments at Alexandria, now in the desert suggest otherwise:

Toda se mudó d'otra figura,
qua non ha panyos nin vestidura.
Perdió las carnes e la color,
que eran blancas como la flor;
los sus cabellos, que eran rubios,
tornáronse blancos e suzios. (lines 720-25)

Tan negra era la su petrina,
como la pez e la resina.
En sus pechos non abiá tetas,
como yo cuido eran secas. (lines 736-39)

Everything about her figure changed,
who has neither clothes nor garment.
She lost her condition and her color,
that use to be white like the flower;
her hair, which used to be blond,

---

[22] The Virgin Mary was also known as the Queen of Heaven in the Christian tradition of the Catholic Church, wherein her presence and influence was in the role of mediator between a grandfatherly rigid God the Father, and her child, or the Son of God; hence, her role as mother.

turned white and dirty.

As black was her breast,
as pitch and resin.
In her chest she did not have breasts,
As I believe they were dry.[23]

Mary is an altered person; physically she no longer is the creature of
beauty with which the poem opens, and who was a lusty creature—desirable
by all men (lines 221-24). Her external beauty was fleeting, and what better
way to show that the predetermined flesh, that external layer of carnal and
secular "appearance," diminishes and wastes away in proportion to the
penance being served. This is a didactic moment of warning. The Church
formula is a simple one; first, [s]he who is able to reflect true, inner beauty
does not need to rely on the external, fleeting appendages of high, physical
appeal. Moreover, the message is that Mary, now the possessor of an older,
yet somehow miraculous body is able to wield a power and influence,
through the dispensation of Divine agency, which culminates in an extended
form of *miraculum*. Indeed, both lines 714-17 and lines 756-59 privilege
Mary's ability to sustain herself for forty years on no more than three pieces
of hard, stone-like bread, which she carried with her from Jerusalem. And
when the bread is finally gone, she is converted into a Nebuchadnezzar-like
beast who eats grass and seeds for eighteen years (lines 774-75).[24] How
does one go about surviving the harshness of the desert in rags, naked,
devoid of creature comfort[s], and still survive, exist and remain penitent?
The poet has privileged Mary as an example of the dispensation of God's
great grace and power. The message—Divine Providence sustains beyond
mere, physical nutrition the vessel that contains the soul.

The poem then leaves Mary and introduces a monk, Don Gozimás
(elsewhere more correctly, Zozimás) (908-11). One day while praying in the
wilderness he sees the figure of María (949). She flees but he follows and
calls out to her to speak to him, which she does saying that she has spent

---

[23] Again, taken together one can distinguish the external beauty of Mary and her
present condition of external, physical disgust and decay; the poet privileges the stark
contrasts that we read in lines 217-24; most notably, that her breasts once compared
to apples in shape and perhaps physical nutrition are now described by the poet: "En
sus pechos non abía tetas / como yo cuido eran secas" ["On her chest she did not
have breasts / As I believe they were dry"] (lines 738-39).
[24] The story of the tragic fall of Nebuchadnezzar's human reasoning in exchange for
an existence as an animal-like herbivore can be found in the Book of Daniel 5:19-21.

forty-seven years in the wilderness as a hermit (979).[25] She then addresses Zozimás by name:

> — Senyor, dixo ella, de Dios amigo,
> muy de grado fablariá contigo,
> que se que buen consejo me darás,
> que tú as nombre Gozimás.
> Mas yo só desnuda creatura
> que non he vestidura ninguna.
> Si uno de tus panyos me diesses,
> yo fablaría lo que quisiesses". (989-96)

> — "Sir, she said, as God is my friend,
> with great pleasure I will speak to you,
> as I know what good counsel you will give me,
> and you have the name Gozimás [Zozimás].
> But I am a naked creature
> who is without any clothing.
> If you would give me one of your garments,
> I will speak that which you desire."

In turn, Zozimás responds in kind, but with some apprehension:

> Cuand' Gozimás se oyó nombrar
> sopo que Dios la fazié fablar,
> ca ella non sabié su nombre
> sinon gelo dixiesse un homne
> Vio que Santi Spiritus gelo mostró
> aquello que ella fabló.
> El santo omne bien se asenyó,
> huno de sus panyos después le dio.
> A la otra parte se tornó
> fasta que la duenya fue vestida,
> contra ell omne santo fizo venida. (997-1008)

> When Zozimás heard his name uttered
> he knew is was God who made her speak,
> because she would not have known his name
> unless some man had told her
> he saw that the Holy Spirit had revealed itself to her [Mary]
> that which she had spoken.
> The holy man understood well,

---

[25] This means that one figures given lines 714-17 and line 749 are not to be taken cumulatively.

one of his garments then gave to her.
He turned to one side
until the Lady was dressed,
towards the holy man she turned.

This trepidation from Zozimás upon hearing his name was enough to turn such anxiety into fear, but he seemingly was given a dispensation of grace to comprehend and understand that Mary, existed as an agent of divine power; again, such *miracula* involving the naming of a saintly monk whom Mary had not met, is commensurate with our earlier chapters, which analyzed the use of *beneficium* within the parameters of "white" magic distinguishable from the dark arts, because of the source of its power. After Mary is fully clothed she offers a response to Zozimás' faith stating:

—"Senyor, dixo ella, amigo de Dios,
¿de cuál parte venides vos?
Por Dios vos ruego que me digades,
¿de cuál parte venides o qué buscades?
Que fe aquí huna doliosa,
que por ell yermo va rencurosa
por los pecados que fizo grandes,
que son tan suzios e tan pesantes,
de que he yo gran repitençia
e só aquí en penitencia." (1009-18)

—Sir, she said, friend of God,
From where have you come?
By God I beseech you to tell me,
From where have you come or what are you up to?
And here is a sorrowful one,
who through the desert space goes sorrowful,
on account of the great sins I have done
that are so dirty and so overwhelming,
of which I have great repentance
and I am here in penitence."

At one point Mary turns towards the East in prayer pleading:

Tornó sus ojos a oriente,
alçó sus manos, al çielo las tiende;
los lambros de la boca movié,
mas nulla boz non le sallié.
De tierra fue allí alçada
que bien hobo una pasada,
así que entre ella e la tierra

dos pies e medio eran. (1104-11)

She turned her eyes toward the East,
Raised her hands, raises them to heaven;
the lips of her mouth moved,
but no sound escaped.
Off the ground she was levitating
So that it was fully the length of a stride,
there between her [Mary] and the ground
two feet and a half was the measure.

Such levitation is a supernatural occurrence, and given the prayer that she "utters," Mary presents another element of "white" magic before Zozimás. Moreover, Zozimás becomes afraid at Mary's ability to levitate, but she calms his fears and asks of him a great favor; the goodwill Mary requests involves that he bring the Blessed Sacrament with him next year at this time to the banks of the Jordan (1191-218). A year later bringing the Blessed Sacrament with him Zozimás comes to the river bank:

Don Gozimás a andar se priso,
un poco de çebada e lentejas consigo.
De flum Jordán, a la ribera
allá priso carrera:
a María cuidó fallar
mas non la hí uvió llegar.
"Dios—dixo—en que yo creyo,
déxame ver lo que deseyo".
A la otra parte la vio estar,
luego comiença de fablar:
—"Duenya, dixo Gozimás,
cara mi madre, ¿qué farás?"
Cuando María lo oyó fablar,
de nulla res non querié dubdar.
Sobr'ell agua vinié María,
com' si viniese por una vía;
a la ribera vino ensucha;
don Gozimás luego la saluda;
a los sus piedes luego se echó,
su bendición le demandó. (1235-54)

Don Zozimás set out travelling,
a little barley and some lentils with him.
To the river Jordan, to it bank
There set out walking:
He tried to find Mary

but there he did not find she had arrived.
"Oh God—he said—in whom I believe,
Show me what I desire."
On the other side he saw her to be,
immediately he begins to speak:
—"Lady, Zozimás said,
dear one, my mother, what will you do?
When Mary heard him speak,
She did not wish him to doubt at all.
Over the water came Mary,
as if she traveled over a dry road;
she arrived dry on the other bank;
the venerable Zozimás immediately welcomes her;
at her feet he immediately threw himslf,
her blessing he demanded.

Mary is given power to walk on water and to arrive at the side of the bank where Zozimás eagerly awaited her; upon recognizing her *miraculum*, he notices she is dry and begins to worship her at her feet, pleading of her, a blessing. The poet suggests that before such "white" magic, it is proper for the saintliest of men to grovel and plead and recognize their status as subservient before such *art*; in short, her walking on water is a *super*natural occurrence, and proceeds toward producing the performance of obeisance from Zozimás. Moreover, after having received the sacrament Mary returns to the desert charging Zozimás to come and look for her a year later alive or dead. Alas, it is to be in death—for Mary dies and the angels take her soul to heaven. Returning at the appointed time Zozimás, finds the corpse of Mary and the admonition written in letters scraped in the ground that he should bury the body (1373-78). It is with great difficulty that the frail, old Zozimás begins the task of digging the grave:

El alma es de ella sallida,
los ángeles la han recebida;
los ángeles la van levando
tan dulce son que van cantando.
Mas bien podedes esto jurar,
que el diablo no y pudi llegar.
Esta duenyaa da enxemplo
A todo omn' que es en este sieglo. (lines 1333-40)

mas por amor d'esta María,
grant ayuda Dios le envia:
salió un leyón d'esa montanya,
a Gozimás faze companya; (lines 1385-88)

El leyón cava la tierra dura,
el santo le muestra la mesura. (lines 1397-98)
Her soul has departed from her,
the angels have received it;
the angels are carrying it
such a sweet sound as they are singing.
But one can well assure this,
That the devil was not able to come there.
This woman provides an example
to all mankind which is in this world.

But for love of this Mary,
God sends him great help:
a lion came out from that wilderness,
to Zozimás he made him company;

The lion digs the hard dirt,
the venerable one [Zozimás] shows him the correct
dimensions.

The representation of the lion as an assistant grave digger is reminiscent of the character of Christ as holding the title, "The Lion of Judah,"[26] and again this naming plays into the theology of the poet as writer and orchestrator of Church authority. Further, God as provider even in death is an echoing theme throughout this poem; moreover, God's power over a beast of prey, ordering it to co-exist with mankind is nothing shy of a *miraculum*. Evidently, if the Church relied on *miracula* to express the explanation of phenomena, and this is distinguished from say, other "arts" because of the source of the dispensation, then the *Vida* belongs to this example. The text privileges a worldly woman who enjoys the favor of God as the result of her austerities. In creating a story such as our poet has done where the beauty of a woman, itself a type of power, although presented as more of a trap than anything else, is trumped by an inner beauty that excels via God's method of penance, the poet is arguing that God, who can forgive anyone, is playing for keeps when it comes to the soul. Mary of Egypt's soul departs, but not until she is fully penitent and has lived out her penance with obedience. The ending of the poem returns in part to the sermonizing charge at the beginning, and utilizes the character of Zozimás, the venerable monk to do so. Zozimás and the lion return to the Monastery of St. John:

---

[26] The title ascribed to the Christ as "The Lion of Judah" is taken from Revelations [or the Book of the Apocalypse] 5:1-7.

Don Gozimás comienca a fablar,
non se quiso más çelar;
de la Egipçiana que non se le olvida,
bien les contó toda su vida; (1423-26)

Don Zozimás began to tell the story,
he did not wish to hide it anymore;
of the Egyptian woman whom he did not forget,
told well all of her life.

These parts of the last 30 or so lines capture the essence of Mary's purposeful life; i.e. her exemplary life applied to all, and that we would do well to remember the Saint because: "…ella ruegue al Criador / con qui ella hobo grant amor," ["she prays to the Creator / for whom she had great love"] (1443-45). The poem's final exhortation, toward a mimetic, penitent life, is an entreaty from Zozimás, the Church and of course the voice of God, wherein sin is regarded as a separator and God's conditions for repentance are rewarded, even in death. As we conclude our analysis on the *Vida*, Jennifer M. Corry reiterates her position concerning the interpretation of magic along the lines of Church subjectivity, namely that which pertains to *miracula*. She states, "The Church believed that it had to compete with magical practice and as a result, created its own counterbalance of Christian 'magic'" (*Perceptions* 137). She positions her explanation of Church authority concerning such a poem as the *Vida* and its saintly protagonist as a didactic example wherein, "the Church was able to suggest the immensity of God's power," as well as suppress and downplay the role of a woman's sexuality by suggesting: "She [Mary] must lose her sexuality and definition as a woman in order to qualify for sainthood under the aegis of the masculine God" (138). Still, a feminist reading, as Corry posits here, is just another example of a modernist's approach toward a thirteenth century Medieval Spanish poem, and the pitfalls for exclusivist and rigid reading equally subjective.

Jointly, the *Auto* and the *Vida* help to position the ever-oscillating and heavily ambiguous subject of *magic* in literature, couched in the explained phenomena of the Church *miracula*; the former poem expressed the duality of magic and science, specifically astrology; the latter poem, a "magic" working within acceptable bounds, or rather belief. The *Vida* is replete with explanations of what the Church would call *miracula*, or what Jennifer M. Corry might suggest were examples of "white" magic. The anonymous poet's protagonist, Mary, surely is a type of wielder of such influence and power, and given the context of the overall poem, the *Vida* suggests a didactic message and calls for a staunch adherence to moral behavior. A community reading such a text is bound to its moral offering[s] and the place that phenomena privileges within the poem, albeit in the form of *miracula*, may be commensurate with an accepting society where such "explanations" of phenomena were couched in their belief and belief systems. Arguably, one might expect that a responsible community would recognize the position of the supernatural in the poem. In the arena that fashioned and shaped the thirteenth century Iberian Peninsula, amidst the study of magic in an amalgamated and heterogeneous culture, these two poems, the *Auto* and the *Vida*— serve, for this project's scope, a small sample of the possible literary contributions toward explaining one's world view; i.e. the position of the [un]seen in the explanation of phenomena.

The society then that mixed language, foods, clothing, intellectual history, translations of Arabic, Greek, and Latin texts into the Castilian language for which Toledo and Córdoba benefited immensely, and in which the University of Salamanca came to prominence was arguably a distinct period. One might add that this period was one of *tolerancia*, or "tolerance." Further, such a time, I argue, was a "pause" button of sorts for what was to come, namely the Spanish Inquisition that relied on the works of the *Malleus Malleficorum*, or the "Hammer of Witches" by Sprenger and Kramer, and decidedly marked a shift in Europe toward the oppression of women and their agency by means of the paranoia of witchcraft, a subject closely linked to this project's examination of magic; but it does not fit its present structure nor its scope. What is more, though this project's compass does not include such an investigation of witchcraft, the author recognizes its impact, and for the present, the subject shall be left for another researcher. For now, the examination of Medieval Spanish Literature with reference to magic and its tolerant practices—for a time—is of present importance.

REFERENCES

Alvar, Manuel, ed. *Vida de Santa Maria Egipciaca*, 2 vols. Madrid: Consejo Superior de Investigaciones Cientificas, 1970-1972.

Álvarez, Ana María López, ed. *La Escuela de Traductores de Toledo.* Toledo: Diputación Provincial de Toledo, 1996.

Ankerloo, Bengt and Stuart Clark, ed. *Witchcraft and Magic in Europe*, 6 vols. Philadelphia: University of Pennsylvania Press, 1999-2002.

Augustine. *De Doctrina Cristiana*, transl. R.P.H. Green. Oxford: Oxford University Press, 1997.

—. *City of God.* Trans. Henry Scowcroft Bettensen. Harmindsworth: Penguin, 1984.

Auto de Los Reyes Magos, Biblioteca Nacional de Madrid, Ms. Vit. 5-9 (*olim* Hh-105), Fol. 67-68^V. *http://64.233.167.104/search?q=cache:kzyrafdkjcij:www.art.man.ac.uk/ spanish/ug/documents/autrrmag_002.pdf+%22auto+de+los+reyes+ma gos%22&hl=en&ct=clnk&cd=12&gl=us*) retrieved 2 August 2007.

Bailey, Michael D. *Battling Demons: Witchcraft, Heresy, and Reform in the Late Middle Ages.* University Park, PA: Pennsylvania State University Press, 2003.

—. "*The meanings of magic.*" *magic, ritual, and witchcraft* 1.1 (Summer 2006): 1(23). *Expanded Academic ASAP.* Thomson Gale. Salem State College. 16 July 2007 <http://find.galegroup.com/itx/infomark.do?&contentSet=IACdocument s&type=retrieve&tabID=T002&prodId=EAIM&docId=A150743483&s ource=gale&userGroupName=mlin_n_state&version=1.0>

Baist, Gottfried. *Das altspanische Dreikönigsspiel: El Misterio de los reyes magos.* Erlangen: A. Deichert, 1887

Bakhouche, Béatrice et al., ed. and trans. *Picatrix: Un traité de magie medieval.* Turnhout: Brepols, 2003.

Baroja, Julio Caro. *Vidas Magicas e Inquisicion*, 2 vols. Madrid: Taurus, 1967.

Barzun, Jacques. *The House of Intellect.* New York: Harper & Row, 1961.

Burns, S.J., Robert I., ed., Samuel Parsons Scott, trans. *Las Siete Partidas*, 5 vols. Philadelphia: University of Pennsylvania Press, 2001.

Bronowski, J. *Magic, Science, and Civilization.* New York: Columbia University Press, 1978.

Callcott, Frank. *The Supernatural in Early Spanish Literature: Studies in the Works of the Court of Alfonso X, El Sabio.* New York: Instituto de las Espanas, 1923.

Clark, Stuart. *Thinking with Demons: The Idea of Witchcraft in Early Modern Europe.* Oxford: Clarendon Press, 1997.

Cohn, Norman. *Europe's Inner Demons: An Enquiry Inspired by the Great Witch-Hunt.* New York: Basic Books, Inc., 1975.

Collinson, Diané. *Fifty Major Philosophers.* New York: Routledge, 2002.

Constable, Olivia Remie, ed. *Medieval Iberia: Readings from Christian, Muslim, and Jewish Sources.* Philadelphia: University of Pennsylvania Press, 1997.

"Cordoba," *Columbia Encyclopedia*, 6th ed.New York: Columbia University Press, 2001-2004. *www.bartleby.com/65/.* 15 June 2007.

Corry, Jennifer M. *Perceptions of Magic in Medieval Spanish Literature.* Bethlehem, PA: Lehigh University Press, 2005.

De Cruz-Saenz, Michele Schiavone. *The Life of Saint Mary of Egypt: an Edition and Study of theMedieval French and Spanish Verse Redactions.* Barcelona: Biblioteca Universitaria Puvill, 1979.

Douay-Rheims version of the Latin Vulgate: *http://www.catholicfirst.com/searchengine.cfm?action=search*; copyrighted 2000-2006; First; retrieved on 17 June 2007.

Evans, G.R. *Fifty Key Medieval Thinkers.* New York: Routledge, 2002.

Fletcher, Richard. *Moorish Spain.* Berkeley: University of California Press, 2006.

Flint, Valerie I.J. *The Rise of Magic in Early Medieval Europe.* Princeton: Princeton University Press, 1991.

Ford, Jr., G.B. *The Letters of St. Isidore of Seville.* 2nd ed. Amsterdam: Adolf M. Hakkert, 1970.

Frazer, Sir James. *The Golden Bough: A Study in Magic and Religion.* 3rd ed., 12 vols. New York: Macmillan, 1935.

Garossa Resina, Antonio. *Magia y Supersticion en la Literatura Castellana Medieval.* Valladolid: Secretariado de Publicaciones, D.L., 1987.

Graebner, Fritz. *Das Weltbild der Primitiven.* Munich: Ernst Reinchardt, 1924.

Greenia, George D. "Review of *The Lapidary of King Alfonso X the Learned* by Ingrid Bahler," *Hispania*, 83.4 (Dec., 2000): 791-92.

Harvey, L.P. *Islamic Spain 1250 to 1500.* Chicago: University of Chicago Press, 1990.

Huffman, Carl, "Pythagoras", *The Stanford Encyclopedia of Philosophy (Winter 2006 Edition)*, Edward N. Zalta (ed.), URL = *http://plato.stanford.edu/archives/win2006/entries/pythagoras/*

Isidore of Seville. *Etymologiarum siue originum libri xx*, ed. W.M. Lindsay, 2 vols. Oxford: Clarendon Press, 1957. First published 1911.

—.*The Etimologies of Isidore of Seville*. Trans. Stephen A. Barney et al. Cambridge: Cambridge University Press, 2006.

Jolly, Karen Louis. *Popular Religion in Late Anglo Saxon England: Elf Charms in Context*. Chapel Hill: University of North Carolina Press, 1996.

—. "Medieval Magic: Definitions, Beliefs, Practices." Ankerloo and Clark 3: 3-71.

Julio Samso et al. *La Escuela de Traductores de Toledo*. Madrid: Diputación Provincial de Toledo, 1996.

Kee, Howard Clark. *Miracle in the Early Christian World: A Study in Sociohistorical Method*. New Haven: Yale University Press, 1983.

Kieckhefer, Richard. *Forbidden Rites: A Necromancer's Manual of the Fifteenth Century*. University Park, PA: Pennsylvania State University Press, 1998.

—. *Magic in the Middle Ages*. Cambridge: Cambridge University Press, 2000.

Kiesel, William, ed. *Picatrix [Ghayat Al-Hakim]: The Goal of the Wise*. Trans. Hashem Atallah. Volume 1. Seattle: Ourboros Press, 2002.

Kingsley, Peter. *Ancient Philosophy, Mystery, and Magic: Empedocles and Pythagorean Tradition*. Oxford: Clarendon Press, 1995.

Las Siete Partidas, ed. Gregorio Lopez. 3 vols. Madrid: Boletin Oficial del Estado, 1974. First published, Salamanca: Andrea de Portoais, 1555.

Las Siete Partidas according to the Medieval Sourcebook taken from *http://origin.web.fordham.edu/halsall/source/jews-sietepart.html*: 15 June 2007.

Lea, Henry Charles. *A History of the Inquisition of Spain*, 4 vols. New York: AMS Press, Inc., 1966. First published 1906-1907.

Lindberg, David C. *The Beginnings of Western Science: The European Scientific Tradition in Philosophical, Religious, and Institutional Context, 600 B.C. to A.D. 1450*. Chicago: University of Chicago Press, 1992.

—., ed. *Science in the Middle Ages*. Chicago: University of Chicago Press, 1978.

Lindsay, Jack. *Origins of Astrology*. New York: Barnes & Noble, Inc., 1973.

Linehan, Peter. *The Spanish Church and the Papacy in the Thirteenth Century*. Cambridge: Cambridge University Press, 1971.

Loomis, C. Grant. *White Magic: an Introduction to the Folklore of Christian Legend*. Cambridge, MA: The Medieval Academy of America, 1948.

Lloyd, G.E.R. *Magic, Reason and Experience: Studies in the origins and development of Greek Science*. Cambridge: Cambridge University Press, 1979.

Madden, Marie R. *Political Theory and Law in Medieval Spain*. New York: Fordham University Press, 1930.

Madrazo, D. Pedro. *España Sus Monumentos y Artes-Su Naturaleza é Historia: Córdoba*. Barcelona: Editorial de Daniel Cortezo y Co., 1884.

Mariño, Maria Brey. *Alfonso X, Rey de Castilla: Lapidario*. Editorial Castalia: Odres Nuevos, 1968.

Maslama Ben Ahmad., Abul Casim., trans.. *Picatrix: El fin del sabio y el major de los dos medios para avanzar*. Madrid: Editoria Nacional, 1982.

Mauss, Marcel., *A General Theory of Magic*. Trans. Robert Brain .New York: Norton., 1972.

McCluskey, Stephen C. *Astronomies and Cultures in Early Medieval Europe*. Cambridge: Cambridge University Press, 1998.

McKay, Angus. *Spain in the Middle Ages from Frontier to Empire, 1000-1500*. London: MacMillan, 1977.

Menocal, Maria Rosa. *The Ornament of the World: How Muslims, Jews, and Christians Created a Culture of Tolerance in Medieval Spain*. Boston: Little, Brown and Company, 2002.

O'Callaghan, Joseph F. *A History of Medieval Spain*. Ithaca: Cornell University Press, 1975.

—. *The Learned King: The Reign of Alfonso X of Castile*. Philadelphia: University of Pennsylvania Press, 1993.

Page, Sophie. *Magic in Medieval Manuscripts*. Toronto: University of Toronto Press, 2004.

—. *Astrology in Medieval Manuscripts*. Toronto: University of Toronto Press, 2002.

Pelikan, Jaroslav. *The Christian Tradition: A History of the Development of Doctrine*, 5 vols. Chicago: University of Chicago Press, 1971-1991.

Peters, Edward. "Superstition and Magic from Augustine to Isidore of Seville." Ankerloo and Clark 3: 175-186.

—. *The Magician the Witch and the Law*. Philadelphia, PA: University of Pennsylvania Press, 1978.

Pingree, David, ed. *Picatrix. The Latin Version of the Ghāyat al-Haleīm*. Studies of the Warburg Institute, 39. London: Warburg Institute, 1986.

Ritter, Hellmut , ed. *Ghayat al-hakim wa-ahaqq al-natijatayn bi-aitaqdim = Das Ziel des Weisen*. Studien der Bibliothek Warberg, 12. Berlin: Teubner, 1933.

Rony, Jerome-Antonie. Bernard Denvir, trans. *A History of Magic*. New York: Walker and Company, 1962.

Sáenz-Badillos, Ángel. "Participación de judíos en las traducciones de Toledo," Álvarez. 65-70.

"Salamanca, city, Spain." *The Columbia Encyclopedia*, 6th ed. New York: Columbia University Press, 2001-04. *www.bartleby.com/65/*. 15 June 2007.

Samso, Julio. "Las traducciones toledanas en los siglos XII-XIII," Álvarez, 17-20.

Scmidt, William. *Der Ursprung des Gottesidee*, 12 vols. Münster: Aschendorf, 1912-1955.

Singer, Charles. *From Magic to Science; essays on the scientific twilight*. London, Benn, 1928.

Stephens, Walter. *Demon Lovers: Witchcraft, Sex, and the Crisis of Belief*. Chicago: University of Chicago Press, 2002.

"taifa," *Encyclopedia Britannica*. 2007. Encyclopdia Britannica Online. 15 June 2007 *http://www.britannica.com/eb/article-9070959*.

Tavenner, Eugene. *Studies in Magic from Latin Literature*. New York: AMS Press, Inc., 1966.

Vallicrosa, José M. Millá. *Las Traducciones orientales en los manuscriptos de la Biblioteca Catedral de Toledo*. Madrid: Instituto Arias Montano, 1942.

Vulgate. *http://www.fourmilab.ch/etexts/www/vulgate/matthew.html*; retrieved on 17 June 2007.

Waxman, Samuel. *Chapters on Magic in Spanish Literature*.Whitefish, MT: Kessinger Publishing, 2007.. First published 1916.

AUTHOR BIOGRAPHY

Francis Tobienne, Jr. was born and raised on the beautiful island of St. Croix, the largest of the three known U.S. Virgin Islands, on 7 July 1975. He attended Trinity College in Deerfield, Illinois and received a Bachelor's degree in Biology/Pre-Medicine with a Secondary in Chemistry, Dean's Scholar 1998. After some consideration, he decided to not continue his medical studies and instead pursued a second degree in English at Michigan State University (MSU), East Lansing, Michigan. It was at MSU that his interest in Medieval & Renaissance Studies began under the auspices of Lister M. Matheson and M. Teresa Tavormina. Upon receiving his second Bachelor's degree in English, he was also able to complete a Master's Degree via distance learning, earning an M.Phil. (*summa cum laude*) with emphasis on Medieval Theology. In 2005, he began work toward his second Master's degree at Purdue University in English, specializing in the area of Literary Studies. On 3 August 2007 he successfully defended his M.A. Thesis at Purdue University, West Lafayette, Indiana. He is currently enrolled in the Ph.D. program in English as a Purdue Doctoral Fellow with continued interest in Medieval & Renaissance Studies, Theory & Cultural Studies. He hopes to continue his academic journey and travels at some point in Spain and in France.